Egyptian Customs
and Festivals

Egyptian Customs and Festivals

Samia Abdennour

The American University in Cairo Press
Cairo • New York

First published in 2007 by
The American University in Cairo Press
113 Kasr el Aini, Cairo, Egypt
420 Fifth Avenue, New York, NY 10018
www.aucpress.com

Dar el Kutub No. 15642/06
ISBN 978 977 416 060 8

1 2 3 4 5 6   12 11 10 09 08 07

Designed by Sarah Rifky
Printed in Egypt

To Hana and Neda
with all my love

Contents

Acknowledgments

I WISH TO express my thanks to Dr. Zeinab Shoosha and Dr. Mahmood Khayal for providing me with valuable information about Islamic traditions.

I am also indebted to Lily Hanna and Dr. Camelia Zaki for their help with Coptic customs.

Last but not least, I wish to thank my husband, Dr. Samir Hanna Sadek, and my daughter, Dr. Soha S. Athanasios, for their critical review of this book and their most valuable additions and suggestions.

Preface

WHAT PROMPTED ME to write this book was an incident involving a western acquaintance of mine. While she meant well, her actions were considered extremely inappropriate by Egyptian standards.

This person heard that her colleague's husband had passed away. Feeling quite upset, she immediately left the office to go and console her friend. Hurrying into the home of the bereaved, she greeted all those present with a loud "Hi!" and in a throbbing voice asked, "What happened? I never knew he was sick," and so on. Her outburst, loud greeting, and dress were all met, to say the least, with a frown by the family and mourners.

So I decided to write the present book to give the western reader a brief description of the Egyptian way of life, customs, and traditions.

Most of the customs described in this book apply to the middle- and upper-middle classes living in the capital and the big cities. The first part of the book deals with a general idea of the mode of life and society, and includes a short summary of etiquette appropriate to various circumstances. The second part deals with religious and non-religious

rites and festivities. The last part is a list of common proverbs and sayings, ending with a list of recipes for some of the foods mentioned in
the book.

I hope this small book will help newcomers to Egypt to appreciate
its culture and avoid any unintended faux pas on their part. I also hope
it will help the children of Egyptian emigrants to the west to understand those aspects of their parents' behavior and ways of thinking
that are alien to their acquired culture.

Introduction

LOOKING AT THE monuments and engravings of the ancient Egyptians, one cannot help noticing how much of the world of the pharaohs is still reflected in present-day life in Egypt. Egyptians are very conservative in their mode of life, and are keen to preserve old rites. Many of the present-day rituals are borrowed from the age-old customs and traditions of the ancient Egyptians. These traditions give modern Egyptians a sense of stability and a feeling of continuity, and for Egyptians who pride themselves on their recorded history of five thousand years, these traditions certainly perpetuate their sense of serenity and security.

The festivities depicted on the monuments show a great similarity to those enjoyed nowadays, whether national or religious, in the merry-making, banquets, dancing, and offering of presents. Although language and religious beliefs have changed radically, the rites bear the imprint of the old pageants. Even the food—vegetables, poultry, fish, or game—is mostly the same as those depicted in tomb and temple decorations.

For many Egyptians life is a daily quest for basic needs, made tolerable because they are comforted by an extended family, consoled by religion, and kept smiling by an irrepressible sense of humor. Egyptians are famous for their jokes and earthy wit. They are friendly, modest, and helpful. They will go out of their way to help foreigners to find their way or invite them for a meal or a glass of tea. Their offers are usually authentic and not proffered in expectation of reward. This generosity is part of their culture and a product of the harsh living conditions, which foster values of sharing and giving.

Egyptians are normally a happy, cheerful people, turning various moments of their lives into song: whether of love, hate, joy, suffering, or desire. Each province has its own poets, songs, dancers, and professional musicians, and Goha, with his cunning and preposterous naiveté, remains the chief buffoon of Egyptian folklore. For many ordinary Egyptians, unsolved problems are usually taken care of with the expression *Khalliha 'ala Allah* ('Leave it to God'). Another 'shock absorber' is *Ma'lish* ('Don't worry,' or 'It's all right'), an essential word in everyone's vocabulary.

Religion plays an essential role in the life of all Egyptians, and is often at the root of their behavior, dress, food, conversation, and dealings. In all social aspects there is no great distinction between Muslims and Copts: the social code is the same except for religious occasions. But religious education is compulsory in all state schools, and the institutions of both faiths work hard to maintain their standing. Both al-Azhar (the oldest Islamic university and an important arbiter of Sunni orthodoxy) and some churches run an entire education system parallel to the state primary and secondary schools. Religious organizations also run clinics and hospitals, as well as sports clubs and other social venues.

Family ties are strong in Egypt, and it is almost unheard of for adult family members to go for months without meeting or visiting each other. Unmarried children live with their parents, irrespective of age. Not only is the cradle-to-grave bond inescapable, it is also inconceivable for Egyptians to live otherwise.

Although a drift into cities and population growth have somewhat altered the sense of community, Egyptians remain extremely family-oriented. Society bestows great reverence on its elders, who are viewed as a *baraka* (blessing), to whom respect and love are due. Respect for elders takes many forms, especially when it comes to body language. In many families, an adult will not sit cross-legged or smoke in front of his or her elders, as both these habits are considered disrespectful. Contradicting an elder's view or raising one's voice in his or her presence is also considered disrespectful. It is not uncommon for an adult to kiss the hand of his or her parents or grandparents as a sign of love and respect. The most common maxims quoted in this respect are *il-'Een mati'lash 'ala-l-hagib* ('The eye does not rise over the brow')—a lesson in humility—and *Akbar minnak bi-yom, a'lam minnak bi-sana* ('Older than you by a day, wiser than you by a year')—an acknowledgment of the wisdom of the elders.

Egyptian society is patriarchal. Fathers hold a position of status and esteem, and are the central figures of authority, the source of the family's reputation, the basis of identity, and the means of economic survival. They are usually the ones who make the decisions in vital issues, such as the children's schooling, their careers, marriage, choice of residence, and so on.

Women, on the other had, both manage the household and participate in the labor force at all skill levels. Their work outside the home has little effect on the division of labor within the house. It is still the woman's role to cook, clean, and raise the children, over and above her work outside the home.

Children are always welcome in Egyptian families. They are considered *Ni'ma min Allah* ('A blessing from God'). Both parents welcome a large number of children, especially boys, who are expected to support them in their old age.

The Egyptian concept of time is very flexible. People will refer to afternoon or evening rather than 4 pm or 9 pm. This is a deeply inherited custom from the days when Egypt was a largely agricultural society, and the daily routine of the Egyptian peasants was defined by sunrise, noon, and nightfall. (Industry—with its more rigid system of punctuality—came much later and has not yet left a strong imprint on the Egyptian way of life.) For a dinner party or a wedding, as a general rule, guests will start showing up no earlier than half an hour after the time set by the hosts.

For everyday entertainment, men largely prefer the company of other men. They usually meet outside the home, in a café or club, to play backgammon or dominoes, drink endless cups of strong, sweet tea, and exchange the latest bawdy jokes. Many women love belly dancing. It is a central part of their culture, and is as much part of their tradition as storytelling. Any joyful occasion is an excuse for them to trill a *zaghruta* (ululation—a high-pitched sound made by flicking the tongue rapidly up and down against the roof of the mouth) and participate in this vital and sensual dance, solo or with others.

All this having been said, there is a tendency nowadays within the younger generation, especially those educated in foreign schools, to do away with old customs and traditions and embrace western habits.

Masr Umm il-Dunya

From time immemorial Egypt has been dubbed *Masr Umm il-Dunya* ('Egypt, Mother of the World'). It was a magnet for talent and learning, as indicated by the importance of the ancient Library of Alexandria, which flourished from the third century BCE to the fourth century CE and to which scientists and men of letters thronged from all parts of the world.

Egypt on the map forms more or less a square of about one million square kilometers, linking Africa to Asia, and subsisting on its artery—the Nile—and its rich fertile soil. Because of its strategic geographical position—it is at the crossing of many trade routes—it has always been the object of foreign greed and conquest.

The population of Egypt is rapidly approaching 72 million, increasing by more than a million every year. Despite numerous land reclamation projects, population growth outstrips the increase in arable land, owing to longer average life expectancy and a decrease in infant mortality, and even in spite of the significant emigration to both the Arab and the western worlds. Apart from the Egyptians, there is a minority of other communities: the Greeks, Italians, Armenians, and so on.

To overcome unemployment and the poor economic conditions in the country, people of all walks of life have been going to the oil-rich Arabian Peninsula seeking work. They have returned home enriched and laden with various electrical appliances: fans, radios, television sets. Since Muslim women were required to wear the veil in these countries, many retained that custom on their return to Egypt. This has created a new class of people very attached to the ultra-conservative values of the Arabian Peninsula, which they believe is a region favored by God through its rich petroleum wells.

Nowadays, one tends to guess the faith of women on the streets of Cairo or other large cities by their dress. Many Muslim women, young and old, have now adopted the veil in its various forms: a head scarf, a dark, all-covering garment, or a middle-length headdress pinned tightly around the face and covering the hair and the arms to the wrist. These are public declarations of modesty and piety, appealing to future mothers-in-law and prospective grooms. At the same time, many Copts tattoo a cross on their wrist or wear a pendant of the cross. Women of both faiths wear dresses or blouses to cover their arms, at least to the elbow.

Most urban men, on the other hand, wear the western dress of shirt and trousers, sometimes a suit and tie, and only enjoy the comfort of the *gallabiya* (a loose garment reaching the ankles, more commonly worn in the villages) when relaxing at home. The young of both faiths, especially those educated in foreign schools, are more interested in imitating western dress. Jeans are very popular—sometimes tight-fitting, shredded at the knees and hems—and are frequently seen protruding under the dresses of veiled girls. Shorts are only tolerated at sports clubs, on the beach, or at home—never in the street.

Cairo is a fascinating city, with striking contrasts standing side by side—modern and ancient monuments, poor and wealthy neighborhoods. Apart from its museums—of antiquities, agriculture, Islamic art, Coptic art, geology, railways, and so on—there are mosques and churches of untold splendor.

Cairo boasts a terrific tourist shopping market, the Khan al-Khalili. The whole of this area is part of medieval Cairo and dates from the thirteenth century. Here tourists delight in strolling through a maze of small alleys and browsing through shops selling copies of pharaonic, Coptic, and Muslim antiquities, embroidered materials, leather, copper, silver and gold jewelry, perfumes, essences, and precious oils. The crucial game here is bargaining, with both tourists and merchants taking the greatest pleasure in sparring and usually ending with both parties delighted with their conquest—the merchant with his sale and the tourist with his or her good deal.

Muslims

Muslims constitute the majority of Egypt's population, numbering about 88 to 90 percent. Most of them are Sunnis, with a small Shi'ite minority.

Islam—the word means 'submission'—is the official religion of Egypt, and its symbol is the crescent moon. The religion has a profound influence on the lifestyle of the country in most aspects, especially in regard to the law, which is based on both *Shari'a* (Islamic law) and the Napoleonic Code.

The Quran, the holy book of Islam, is regarded as immutable and infallible, as are the *Hadith* (the sayings of the Prophet) and the *Sunna* (precepts based on the example of the Prophet's life). The Quran constitutes the alpha and omega of Islamic thought, spiritual and ethical teachings, and artistic manifestations. It is written in Arabic, which Muslims consider the only authorized language to be used in their religious rites throughout the world, regardless of what the local language may be. The Quran is the sum of God's revelations to the Prophet Muhammad through the Archangel Gabriel over a period of twenty-two years beginning in 610 CE. These revelations were passed on orally by the Prophet Muhammad to his followers, who codified them in 651. Since then, no changes whatever have been introduced.

The Five Pillars of Islam, to which all believers must adhere, are:

al-Shahada (testimony): To declare publicly and sincerely: *La ilaha illa Allah, Muhammad rasul Allah* ('There is no god but

God, Muhammad is the Prophet of God'). Anyone
proclaiming these words is accepted as a Muslim.

al-Salat (prayer): To pray five times a day at *fajr* (dawn), *dhuhr*
(noon), *'asr* (afternoon), *maghrib* (sunset) and *'isha*
(evening), facing the *qibla* (direction of Mecca).
Prayers should be preceded by *wudu'* (ablution).

al-Sawm (fasting): To fast for the entire month of Ramadan—
no food or drink, impure thoughts, or sexual relations are allowed from sunrise to sunset (for more
information, see page 74). Some of the faithful also
fast every Monday and Thursday in the other
months of the year.

al-Hajj (pilgrimage): Every Muslim should make the pilgrimage
to Mecca at least once, as long as he or she can
afford it and is in good enough health to go. Upon
the pilgrim's return, he or she assumes the title of
Hagg or Hagga (for more information, see page 80).
If ill-health prevents the faithful from performing
the pilgrimage, a second party may perform it on his
or her behalf.

al-Zaka' (tithe): This is considered an obligatory tax and is calculated as *rub' al-'ushr* (a quarter of a tenth, or 2.5
percent) of one's income, to be distributed to the
poor. It can be paid at one's own discretion, either
by installments or at one go. However, the *zaka'*

should not be confused with *sadaqa* (alms), which is
required of all well-to-do Muslims, to be given
freely.

The religious offices in Sunni Islam are: the *mufti* (chief religious advis-
er or legislator), *'alim* (teacher), *shaykh* (clerk), *fiqi* (Quran reciter), and
imam (prayer leader).

Muslims hold piety to be the greatest of virtues. They invoke God's
name in all their dealings and conversation. Men may display their
piety through their *zibiba* (prayer bruise on the forehead) and *sibha*
(rosary), which they publicly hold, counting the beads and all the while
reciting verses from the Quran. Their greeting is *al-Salamu 'alaykum*
('Peace be upon you'), at whatever time of day or night.

Although Friday is the day of rest, Muslims are not forbidden to
work, but are only required to desist from any worldly occupation at
noon so that they can perform the midday prayer with its four *rak'at*
(prostrations), preferably at the mosque, and to listen to the *khutba*
(sermon) of the *khatib* (orator).

Prayers at home are performed on a *siggadat sala* (prayer rug) for the
able, or seated on a chair for those unable to prostrate. Men and
women must remove their footwear before praying, and before enter-
ing a mosque, while women are also required to have everything but
their face and hands covered during prayer. When praying in the
mosque, women must pray behind a curtain or on a balcony shielded
from the men. They gain access to their place of worship through a
private entrance.

Praying in the mosque on Fridays at noon, and at dawn on the *Id*s is highly recommended, though not compulsory. Most mosques are too small to hold the number of people coming to pray, and mats are therefore spread on adjoining sidewalks or in the street to accommodate the faithful. A common sight on Friday noon is men of all social classes sitting cross-legged side by side on these mats in the street to pray and hear the sermon that follows the prayer.

The mosque is completely devoid of furniture, with the exception of carpets, chandeliers, and the *minbar* (pulpit). The walls are bare of pictures, and the only adornments are verses from the Quran, written in beautiful calligraphy, and uniform geometric designs. The prohibition of figurative imagery in religious buildings is to avoid idolatry.

The mosque is a house of prayer, but it welcomes those who merely want to enjoy its serenity. Unlike churches, where only prayers are held, mosques often host other scenes: a sheikh quietly giving a religious lesson to students seated cross-legged on a carpet; a poor man sleeping peacefully behind a column; a young student with his academic books spread around him enjoying the peaceful haven of the mosque. These are all accepted norms.

Food for Muslims is either *halal* (permissible) or *haram* (forbidden). Among items that are *halal* are seafood, all plants, and herbivores that are slaughtered by a single knife stroke across the jugular, with the words *Bismillah, Allahu akbar* ('In the name of God, God is greatest'). Pork and the flesh of carnivores, reptiles, insects, and animals found dead are *haram*. When eating with the fingers, only the right hand should be used.

Strictly forbidden under Islam are pictures personifying the Prophet Muhammad, alcoholic beverages, usury, and gambling. In addition, women should not fast, pray, or handle the Quran during menstruation.

A very popular Islamic amulet, originally Shi'ite but now accepted by all Muslims, is the *khamsa wi-khmesa,* or the Hand of Fatima, a spread palm showing the five fingers and symbolizing *ahl al-bayt* (the family), that is, the Prophet Muhammad, his daughter Fatima, his son-in-law Ali and his grandsons Hassan and Hussein.

Copts

It could be said that all native Egyptians descended from ancient Egyptian stock are 'Copts,' because the word 'Copt' originally meant 'Egyptian'—of both faiths. 'Copt' comes from the Arabic *qibti*, which derives from the Greek term *aigyptos*, meaning 'Egyptian,' but the term nowadays has come to define specifically the Christian Egyptians.

Though the Copts are very religious, they prefer not to be called the Christians of Egypt, claiming that the epithet 'Copt' eloquently combines their nationality and religion. It also distinguishes them from naturalized Egyptian Christians. Not content that their religion is stamped on their identity cards, many Copts will tattoo a cross on the inside of their right wrist or wear pendant crosses or crucifixes (men placing these under their shirts). This is viewed as a sign of piety and devotion.

The majority of Copts belong to an independent branch of the Eastern Church called the Coptic Orthodox Church. It broke from the Eastern Church in the fifth century and since then has maintained its autonomy. Its beliefs and rituals have remained basically unchanged. There are also other groups of Copts, mainly Protestants of different denominations and Catholics, who have their own churches and rituals, but they constitute only a minority. Their religious rites differ from those of the Orthodox Church, but not their civil customs and traditions, which are similar to those of all Egyptians.

There are no exact statistics showing the number of Copts, but a rough estimate of ten percent of the population is considered close. Over the centuries many adopted Islam, while others, especially in the last fifty years, have emigrated to the west. In language and way of life they are indistinguishable from their compatriots, the Muslims. They have survived as a religious entity, but otherwise are completely integrated in the body politic of the nation, sharing privileges, traditions, and responsibilities.

The Coptic language is the last phase in the evolution of the language of the ancient Egyptians. To this day Copts, whose native language is Arabic, have retained the use of Coptic as a liturgical language in the Coptic Orthodox Church. A very small minority of Copts read or understand Coptic.

Calendars

Herodotus, visiting Egypt in the fifth century BCE, said: "The Egyptian calendar is certainly the only rational calendar that has ever been devised."

The ancient Egyptians were one of the first nations to use a solar calendar, in around 3000 BCE, which shows their great regard for science and the high level of knowledge they attained. Their calendar was based on the phases of the River Nile and their associated activities in the fields: Inundation, Seedtime, and Harvest—three distinct seasons of four months each. These seasons shaped the life and character of the Egyptian fellaheen (peasants), who were so engrossed in agriculture and their land that they left all other matters—social, political, and economic—to outsiders. It was this that facilitated foreign control of the country and led to the peasants' eventual oppression.

Egyptians nowadays use three calendars: the Islamic, the Coptic (descended from the ancient Egyptian), and the western calendar, which is used by both faiths for most secular or official purposes. The Islamic calendar is used only for religious purposes, while the Coptic calendar is used to mark the events of the Christian year and—by farmers of both faiths—the agricultural almanac. The names given to the Islamic months were largely adopted from those of the *Jahiliya* (the 'time of ignorance,' that is, the period before Islam), while the names of the Coptic months are derived from the names of ancient Egyptian gods or festivals. Thus Tut commemorates Thoth, the god of wisdom, while Hatur corresponds to Hathor, the goddess of love and fertility.

The Islamic Calendar

The origins of the Islamic calendar lie in the beginning of the fifth century CE, with the Arabs of the *Jahiliya*. The calendar is lunar, with the months calculated according to the appearance of the new moon. There are twelve months in the calendar, each varying between 28 and 30 days, with a total of 354 days. The months were originally named according to tribal needs and prevailing current events, but when Islam came to the Arabian Peninsula the *Jahiliya* calendar was not abandoned. Although these months move in relation to the solar year, and therefore do not reflect their meanings at all times, their names are still used up to the present.

The Islamic calendar, called the *Hijra* ('migration') calendar, started in 622 CE, the year the Prophet Muhammad moved from Mecca to Medina, and is identified by the abbreviation AH. Because this calendar is lunar and is eleven days shorter than the solar year, months and holidays appear to rotate around the western calendar.

The months (and the original meanings of their names) are:

Muharram ('Forbidden'). The first month of the lunar calendar. On 10 Muharram, 'Ashura ('the tenth') commemorates the death of Imam Hussein, the grandson of the Prophet. A special dish of boiled wheat with milk, nuts, and raisins called *'ashura* is traditionally served on this day.

Safar ('Departure'—people travel away from the heat to look for food).

Rabi' al-Awwal ('Spring I'—when the plants start to grow). On
            the 12th of this month Muslims celebrate Mulid al-
            Nabi, the Prophet's birthday (see page 73).
Rabi' al-Thani ('Spring II').
Jumada al-Awwal ('Frozen I'—this month originally fell in win-
            ter, when the water, a rare and precious commodity
            in the desert, froze).
Jumada al-Thani ('Frozen II').
Rajab (in the Cairo dialect, Ragab). On 27 Ragab, Muslims
            celebrate Laylat al-Isra' wa-l-Mi'raj ('night of the
            nocturnal journey and ascent'). This night com-
            memorates the Prophet's journey from Mecca to
            Jerusalem, then his ascension to the heavens and
            return to Mecca, all in one single night, riding al-
            Buraq, a winged creature. The rock from which he
            ascended to heaven in Jerusalem is now housed
            under the Dome of the Rock, one of the holiest of
            Islamic places. This month, with Dhu-l-Qi'da,
            Dhu-l-Hijja, and Muharram, is one of *al-Ushhur al-
            haram* ('the months of prohibition'), because war is
            prohibited during these four months. A proverb
            says *'Ish Rajaban, tara 'ajaban* ('Live Rajab and you
            will see wonders').
Sha'ban ('Disperse'—when the people disperse looking for
            water). On 14 Sha'ban the Prophet Muhammad

began the preparations for Ramadan, on Laylat
Nuss Sha'ban ('the night of mid-Sha'ban). Muslims
fast on the 15th.

Ramadan ('Intense heat'—stones are said to became fiery
from the heat). It is said of this month of daylight
fasting (see page 74), "When Ramadan comes the
gates of Heaven open and the gates of Hell close."
Notwithstanding its solemnity, the month is spent
in gaiety, equality, and fraternity. Laylat al-Qadr ('the
Night of Destiny'), whose precise date is not
known but falls during the last ten days of
Ramadan, is conventionally celebrated on the 27th.
It commemorates the Prophet's review of the entire
Quran, and is said to be *Khayr min alf shahr* ('Better
than a thousand months'). At the end of Ramadan
Muslims celebrate 'Id al-Fitr ('The Feast of the
Breaking of the Fast').

Shawwal ('Decrease'—during this month the camel's milk
decreases).

Dhu-l-Qi'da ('The month of sitting down'—the month of forbidden war).

Dhu-l-Hijja ('The month of pilgrimage'). The pilgrimage to
Mecca takes place in this month. A special dress of
seamless white cloth called the *ihram* is worn by
both sexes. The rituals culminate on 10 Dhu-l-Hijja

with 'Id al-Adha ('The Feast of the Sacrifice'; see page 80).

Some boys born during the months of Sha'ban, Ragab, and Ramadan will be given these names as a sign of devotion and gratitude for the birth of a boy.

The Coptic Calendar

Year 1 of the Coptic calendar is 284 CE, the year Diocletian became emperor in Rome, and is identified by the abbreviation AM, for Anno Martyrum, the Year of the Martyrs. Diocletian's reign is noted for the torture and mass executions of Christians, especially in Egypt.

The Coptic year is divided into thirteen months, twelve months of thirty days each, with the thirteenth month comprising five (or six if it is a leap year) intercalary days called Nasi ('Forgotten') to complete the 365 days of the year.

The Coptic calendar is used by farmers of both faiths in their cycle of seeding and harvesting crops. The peasants have attached an adage to every month that rhymes with its name and describes its character.

The names and adages of these months are:

Tut (from Thoth, god of wisdom) starts 11 September. *il-Katkut
        yakul wi-ymut* ('The chick eats and dies'): during this
        month chicks are likely to become diseased and die.
        Nayrouz, or Coptic New Year, falls on 1 Tut, when

the Nile starts to rise. It is interesting to note here
that although the rites are believed to be pharaonic,
the appellation is Iranian—Nayrouz in Persian means
New Year.

Baba starts 11 October. *Udkhul wi-'fil il-bawaba* ('Enter and
close the gate'): get inside and keep out the cold.

Hatur (from Hathor, goddess of love and fertility) starts 10
November. *Abu-l-dahab il-mantur* ('The month of the
golden spread'): the wheat is ripe and golden in
color. The advent fasting period starts on 16 Hatur,
25 November.

Kiyahk starts 10 December. *Sabahak masak* ('Your morning is
your evening'): the day is very short. On 29 Kiyahk,
7 January, Copts celebrate Christmas, which is now
an official holiday enjoyed by all Egyptians.

Tuba starts 9 January. *Tisir il-sabiya karkuba* ('The lass becomes
a hag'): maidens cringe and shrivel like old women
because of the cold weather. Coptic Epiphany is 11
Tuba, 19 January. The end of this month is marked
by strong winds called *zaffit Amshir* ('the announcement of *Amshir*').

Amshir starts 8 February. *Abu-l-za'abib il-kitir* ('The month of
many strong winds') and *Ti'ul li-l-zar' sir sir* ('Tell the
plants to grow'): the shoots start appearing and grow-
ing. On 6 Amshir, 13 February, Copts fast for three

days in memory of Jonah being swallowed by the
whale. During this month and the month that follows,
hot, humid winds laden with desert sand, the *khamasin*
('fifties'—because they occur during these fifty days),
are not uncommon. They usually last for twelve hours,
very rarely more than twenty-four. Visibility during
this period is very poor and many airports and har-
bors are closed, while traffic is at its minimum.

Baramhat starts 8 March. *Ruh il-ghayt wi hat* ('Go to the field
and fetch'): the crops are now ripe and ready for
harvesting.

Barmuda starts 10 April. *Du"u-l-sha'ir bi-l-'amuda* ('Pound the
barley with the rod').

Bashans starts 9 May. *Yiknis il-ghayt kans* ('Sweeps the field clean'):
clear the land and allow it to rest before the new crop.

Ba'una starts 8 June. *La yindirib tub wala yit'imil mona* ('Neither
bricks are formed nor mortar made'): the excessive
heat will affect even bricks and mortar.

Abib starts 8 July. *Illi yakul mulukhiya fi Abib, yigib il-tabib* ('Whoever
eats *mulukhiya* during Abib must call the doctor'):
mulukhiya—Jew's mallow, a leafy vegetable very popular
in Egypt—is in its very early stage of growth and cannot be differentiated from harmful weeds.

Misra ('Birth of the Sun') starts 7 August. *Tigri kull tir'a 'asira*
('Every dry canal is filled'): during this period the

flood inundates the land, filling all the dry canals.
Fifteen days' fasting begins on 1 Misra, 7 August, in
honor of the Virgin Mary, whose feast is on 15
Misra, 22 August.

Nasi starts 6 September.

Coptic Festivals:

January 7	Christmas
January 19	Epiphany
February 13	Fast of Jonah (3 days)
June 11	Pentecost
June 12	Fast of the Apostles
July 12	Feast of the Apostles
August 7	Fast of the Virgin
August 22	Feast of the Virgin
September 11	Coptic New Year
November 25	Fast of Advent

Lent, Palm Sunday, and Good Friday have no fixed dates and vary according to the date fixed for Coptic Easter. *Shamm al-Nisim*, a spring festival
celebrated by both Copts and Muslims, occurs on the Monday following
Coptic Easter.

Customs and Traditions

Names

Egyptians are generally known by three names: the name given to them at birth, their father's name, and their grandfather's name. Thus Samir Hanna Sadeq denotes the name given to the infant, Samir; his father's name, Hanna; and his grandfather's name, Sadek.

A small number of Egyptians have surnames or family names. The origin of this custom dates back to the nineteenth century. Muhammad Ali, viceroy of Egypt (1811–49), appropriated all the land of the country and became its sole owner. However, as a reward for various services rendered he bestowed gracious endowments on a few of his subjects in the form of land. These individuals became feudal landlords, and on their death their offspring naturally inherited the land. To emphasize their claim of ownership, these heirs retained the name of the original recipient and thus became known as the family Badrawi, Doss, and so on. Thus until today the concept of acquiring land through inheritance, as opposed to buying it, is stamped with the hallmark of prestige, prosperity, and good background.

Names sometimes bear a religious identity: Ragab, Ramadan, Sha'ban (names of Islamic months), Muhammad, Hassan, and Zeinab are undoubtedly Muslim names, while Boctor, Kirollos, and Dimyana are distinctly Coptic. It is also common in Muslim families to register two names as a first name on their son's birth certificate, starting with the Prophet's name, then following it with the chosen name. Thus in a family of two sons the birth certificates may read Muhammad Hosni and Muhammad Anwar, although the boys will be known as Hosni and Anwar. Meanwhile, some Coptic families will choose as a name for their newborn the first name they come across on opening the Bible at random. For this reason, names like Esther, Israel, and Rachel are not uncommon among Copts.

Names in Arabic usually have a meaning. They may be epithets like Karim ('generous') and 'Adel ('righteous') or a humble attribute to God such as 'Abd al-Muntasir ('slave of the Victorious'), 'Abd al-Hafez ('slave of the Preserver'), and so on. As a result of travels and conquests, other foreign names, mainly Turkish, Persian, and British, have also infiltrated the naming rules and have become popular with the Egyptian community. Thus 'Esmat and Mervat are Turkish names, Safinaz and Nermin are Persian, while William and Victoria are definitely British.

Names are always written in full—that is, the three names: the child's, the father's, and the grandfather's or the family name—and initials are not used in Arabic. Although officially a person has three names, he or she is commonly known by only two. As a second name, some people will prefer to use their grandfather's name over their father's and will attach it to their names, omitting the father's name. This can naturally cause confusion, especially for westerners, as siblings will then have different second names, and outsiders are at a loss to understand the family link between them. For example, flautist Inas 'Abd al-Dayem is the sister of soprano Iman Mustafa; writer Mursi Saad Eddin is the brother of composer Baligh Hamdi; and musician Mursi Gamil is the brother of singer Fayda Kamel. To overcome this ambiguous situation some families—mainly in the middle and upper-middle classes—have recently started adopting the grandfather's name as a family surname.

Under all circumstances, women officially retain their maiden names after marriage and do not automatically assume their husbands'. This is a Muslim doctrine applicable to all women of both faiths and is related to ownership of property and the protection of women's rights. However, on the social level and as an exception to the rule, the presidents' wives, Jehan and Suzanne, are known as Jehan Sadat and Suzanne Mubarak.

Among the lower classes, some women prefer to conceal their names from strangers, and are called, for example, Umm Karim ('Mother of Karim'), Karim being the first-born son. Such women do not view this as a negation of their identity, but on the contrary are proud of this appellation and feel that it ennobles them. Men too are often pleased to be called, for example, Abu Karim, to show their pride in conceiving a son, although this is less common.

In the immediate aftermath of the July 1952 Revolution—the heyday of secular Pan-Arab nationalism—Egyptians tended to shun names too closely identified with religion, opting instead for names such as Samer ('entertainer') or Soha (the name of a star) that had no obvious religious connotations. Today, however, that tide has been reversed. A name like Islam was never heard of in the early 1950s, yet now it is not uncommon among Muslims, whereas Fadi ('sacrificed'—referring to Christ) is now in vogue among Copts.

Addressing people by their first names is less common in Egypt than in the west. A title—not necessarily merited—frequently precedes the first name. Thus:

- Adults will address one another as *Ustaz* (Mr., literally 'professor') or *Anisa* (Miss) or *Madam* (Mrs.).
- If a person has a professional degree, the first name will be preceded by his or her title: Mohandis ('Engineer') Medhat, Doctor Mona.
- As a mark of respect, a vendor may add *Hagg* or *Hagga* (literally, a person who has been on pilgrimage) before a customer's name, even if he or she has never made a pilgrimage; or they might follow it with *Bey* or *Hanem*, thus conferring a respectable title on this person.
- A friendly epithet of *Abla* ('big sister') or *Abey* ('big brother') sometimes breaks the severity of mere acquaintance, and at the same time keeps a polite distance.

- Children will call any acquaintance of their parents *'Ammu* ('uncle') or *Tante* ('aunt'), rather than Mr. or Mrs., and definitely not by their first name alone.
- An older man of lower social status may be addressed as *'Amm* X ('uncle' X), again to show friendship.
- Children among themselves will address one another as *kabtin* ('captain') if they do not know the other child's name.
- Among the lower classes, women's names are seldom mentioned, and women are usually called *Umm* X ('mother of X'), as mentioned above.

Some Arabic names and their meanings:

Name	*Meaning*
'Adel	Righteous
Amal	Hopes
Amani	Wishes
Amin	Honest
Amira	Princess
'Azmi	My Will
Badr	Full Moon
Bahaa	Glory
Basma	Smile
Bushra	Annunciation
Camelia	a type of flower
Dalal	Coquettishness

Doha	Dawn
Farid	Unique
Faten	Bewitcher, Seducer
Fuad	Heart
Gamal	Beauty
Gamil	Beautiful
Hadil	Cooing of Pigeons
Haitham	Brave Lion
Hana	Health and Happiness
Hassan	Good, Beautiful
Hosni	My Beautiful One, My Good One
Kamal	Perfection
Karam	Generosity
Karim	Generous
Khaled	Eternal
Magdi	My Glory
Maher	Adept
Mahmoud	Thanked
Manal	Aspiration
Nada	Dew
Nargess	Narcissus
Osama	Brave Lion
Rafiq	Friend, Companion
Ragaa'	Entreaty
Reda	Accepting Destiny

A Coptic bride and groom kneeling at the altar. *Photograph by Claudia Yvonne Wiens.*

The name of God—Allah—on a street sign in one of Cairo's main squares. *Photograph by Mohamed El-Masry.*

A Muslim bride and groom dancing at their *zaffa. Photograph by Tod Cross/IBA Media.*

Subu' rituals to commemorate a new birth. *Photograph by Wessam Omar/IBA Media.*

Family members lining up to receive condolences at a funeral. *Photograph by Mohamed El-Masry.*

A traditional amulet used to ward off the evil eye. *Photograph by Ashraf Talaat/IBA Media.*

A street vendor selling *tirmis,* lupine seeds. *Photograph by Mohsen Allam/Egypt Today.*

Serving up a plate of *kushari,* the nutritious mix of pasta, lentils, and rice. *Photograph by Khaled Habib/Egypt Today.*

The grounds of a sprawling *mulid* in Upper Egypt. *Photograph by Claudia Yvonne Wiens.*

A folk dance troupe performing at a *mulid*. *Photograph by IBA Media.*

A street stall selling *mulid* sweets and dolls. *Photograph by Mohamed El-Masry.*

Safaa'	Purity
Sahar	Dawn
Salah	Righteousness
Salma	Safe
Samer	Entertainer
Sawsan	a type of flower
Sherif	Honest
Soha	the name of a star
Suhail	the name of a star
Tarif	Pleasant
Tawfiq	Success
Wadi'	Tame, Gentle
Zaghloul	Chick
Zarif	Pleasant

The Name of God

Egyptians are by nature religious at heart. They are forever invoking God's name at every occasion and circumstance: in love, hate, disapproval, despair, surprise, and so on. Punctuating all conversations with incantations of *In sha' Allah* ('God willing') and *al-Hamdu li-llah* ('thanks be to God') is as natural to an Egyptian as breathing. This is not superstition but a deeply ingrained belief in God's power and a plea for benediction in all matters.

The simple word *Allah* ('God') given different intonation or stress can have many different meanings, and will eloquently replace a whole sentence or expression. Thus, in admiration, the second syllable is stretched to sound like *Allaaaah*; in confusion the word is repeated two or three times: *Allah, Allah, Allah*; while in astonishment, surprise, or perplexity, the stress is on the first syllable: *Aaallah*.

Male names including the word *Allah* abound: Hamdallah, Shukrallah (both meaning 'thanks to God'), and Sa'dallah ('God's happiness'), to name a few. At the same time, names starting with 'Abd ('slave' or 'servant')—such as 'Abd al-Rahim ('slave of the Merciful') and 'Abd al-Mu'ti ('slave of the Giver')—are all expressions of servitude to God.

Muslim women often wear brooches, pendants, or other jewelry bearing the word *Allah* in beautiful calligraphy, accepted as a sign of piety and uprightness. A very popular gift to a newborn Muslim infant is a brooch bearing the word *Allah*—apart from its material value, it is an amulet believed to dispel evil spirits and bless the child.

In many Coptic families, the words *al-Rabb* ('the Lord') or *Rabbina* ('our Lord') replace *Allah*.

The word *Allah* has become such a part of the language that expressions including the name of God abound. Following are some of the most common expressions used, with their meanings:

Allahu akbar ('God is greatest'): Apart from being the opening to the Muslim call to prayer, this expression is used to ward off the evil eye. To express admiration for a child or object without following it with

Allahu akbar or *Ma sha' Allah* ('As God wishes') is
inviting trouble (see the section on Superstition,
below). Copts in this context will use the expression *Bism il-salib* ('In the name of the cross').

Allah yiddilak tult al-'umr ('May God give you long life'), *Allah
yikhallik* ('May God keep you alive'), *Allah yis'idak wi-
ykhallik* ('May God keep you happy and alive') are all
wishes for longevity, and said as a favorable answer,
as thanks, or simply in answer to a greeting.

Allah yigazik ('May God punish you') is said jokingly in reply
to a prank, or with great disappointment when
someone fails to live up to expectation, but of
course with a different tone of voice.

Allah yihfazak or *Allah yikhallik* (both meaning 'May God preserve you') are said to express appreciation or thanks.

Allah yirhamuh/yirhamha ('God have mercy on him/her') is said
when someone dies.

Astaghfar Allah (I ask God's forgiveness') is used to do just
that or to modestly decline a compliment.

Bismillah ('In the name of God') is an expression used as an
opening or foreword before any new venture, whether
a speech, a journey, or a meal. This expression is used
by both Muslims and Copts, unlike *Bismillah al-Rahman
al-Rahim*, which is used only by Muslims. It is
expressed to validate important agreements, to give

courage at times of uncertainty, and to lend auspi-
ciousness to countless daily events. A *Bismillah* is also
used as an invitation to partake of food. Any person,
whether an acquaintance or a stranger, coming upon
another person eating will automatically be invited to
share the food using this expression.

al-Hamdulillah ('Thanks to God') is used at the end of a meal,
or in answer to a question. The reply is the same
whether it is in the affirmative or negative, but the
inflection of the voice determines which is which.
"Do you want another helping?" *Al-Hamdulillah*
(meaning 'No'). "Did you enjoy your outing?" *Al-
Hamdulillah* (meaning 'Yes').

In sha' Allah ('God willing'). It is unheard of to declare an
intention to do something, go somewhere, or even
plan an event without preceding or following it with
In sha' Allah. Even in answer to a question—for
example, is Mr. Sherif going somewhere? Are you
doing anything tomorrow?—when the answer is in
the affirmative, the same expression, *In sha' Allah*, is
used, adding eloquence to the 'yes.'

Ism Allah (God's name) is used both as an invocation to God
for protection—for example, if a person is about to
fall—or, with a different inflection of voice, con-
temptuous astonishment.

Khalliha 'al-Allah ('Leave it to God') is said when a problem is
complicated and does not seem soluble.

Tawakkalna 'al-Allah ('We have placed our trust in God') is
said before starting on a journey or a new project.

Yarhamukum Allah ('May God have mercy on you') is the
expression used when a person sneezes.

Marriage

In Egypt, the peak of the crescendo of life's events is marriage. This
is one of society's major goals. Normally girls become eligible for marriage at the age of 18, and their chances of marriage dwindle as they
approach 30. Men, on the other hand, have no age limit—if they are
young when thinking of marrying, between 25 and 30, they are viewed
as ambitious and eager to shoulder responsibility. If older, they are
described as mature and able to afford a comfortable life for a family,
as is expected of a breadwinner. It is said of an unmarried woman,
Fat-ha il-'atr ('The train has passed her by'), and mention of her name
is usually accompanied by *Rabbina yifukk di'it-ha* ('May God relieve her
of her difficulty').

The traditions binding marriage are very well defined. The parents
are usually the sole authority when it comes to deciding matrimonial
matters. They sit as counselors, judges, and executors of their children's best interests. They shape and control their lives, not just up to
a certain age, but until they leave the parental home (and sometimes
beyond). They choose, accept, or refuse a spouse as they deem fit.

They feel that marriage is too much of a gamble to be left to the judgment of the young.

In many families arranged marriages are the norm and romantic love is frequently a secondary consideration. That is why marriage between relatives is regarded as the most suitable, as it offers the advantage of pairing two individuals of relatively similar background and mutual interests, as against a 'difference in levels' that may serve as a basis for disagreement and conflict. Male cousins claim a prior right to marry female cousins, and refusing a cousin (especially a paternal cousin) because one prefers a stranger can be the cause of a serious family feud.

The first customary step in the marriage procedure is for the parents of the young man to send word, through a mutual acquaintance, to the parents of the young woman requesting the pleasure of visiting them. Before agreeing to this visit, both families make informal inquiries—family background, health, occupation, income, piety, physical attractiveness, and so on—about one another to determine compatibility. Some young couples may not be strangers but may already have met at university, at a club, or at work, and may even have exchanged vows of eternal fidelity. Yet they rarely confront their parents with their decision, but abide by matrimonial dicta—whatever these may decree.

The girl's opinion is normally sought by her parents before they agree to the visit. If she approves of the young man, she may blushingly say *Illi tshufu ya baba* ('Whatever you see fit, daddy'), but if the young man does not live up to her aspirations she can refuse with an excuse like *'Ayzin tikhlasu minni?* ('Do you want to get rid of me?'). An unfavorable yet polite reply from the girl's parents to the parents of the proposed groom would be *Mafish nasib* ('It was not fated'). But if both families agree to the bond, the parents of the young woman will arrange a date to welcome those of the young man.

The young man accompanies his parents on this initial visit to make an official request for her hand. (A request by the groom with-out his parents would be unbecoming, making the bride lose face, under the assumption that his family rejected the union). It is the groom's parents who make the request by saying, *Talbin il-'urb* ('We want to be related to you'), and the reply is, *Yisharrafna* ('It would honor us'). With these preliminary civilities over, the parents recite the opening prayer of the Quran, the *Fatiha*, in the case of Muslims, or *Abana-llazi* (the Lord's Prayer) in the case of Copts. These prayers bind the two families socially and are the first seal on the financial negotiations, which are an important concern to insure the bride's security. They now fix a date for the *khutuba* (engagement).

Before the official engagement takes place, the groom declares the amount he will allocate to buy jewelry for his prospective bride as a *shabka* (bond). The more expensive the *shabka*, the more the bride feels that the groom cherishes her and adds to her stature. The groom, bride, and members of both families will select and buy the jewelry they decide will be fit for the occasion: rings (which represent mutual love and affection flowing from one to the other) and other items such as bracelets, earrings, and pendants. The groom will present the *shab-ka* to his bride-to-be at the engagement party.

During the engagement period it is customary for the groom to shower his fiancée with presents, which she must treasure carefully until she moves to her new home. If the bride breaks the engagement, she must return all the presents given to her by her fiancé or his family and friends during the period of the *khutuba*. However if the groom breaks the engagement, he is not entitled to any reimbursement. During this period the couple fix a date for their wedding ceremony.

These are the preliminary steps that both Muslims and Copts adhere to before shouldering the other religious and financial responsibilities. Then there are further stages, which differ between the two religious communities.

Muslims

Muslims have a clear code of matrimonial financial obligation. While the bride's father promises to provide his daughter with an adequate trousseau and most of the requirements of the household, the groom must provide all electrical appliances and declare the amount he is prepared to pay for the *shabka* as well as the *mahr* (dowry).

The *mahr* is a two-part payment: the *mu'addam* (advance payment) and the *mu'akhkhar* (delayed payment). Again, the value of the *mahr* reflects the esteem the groom has for his future wife, and also assures the girl's parents of her security. The *mu'addam* is an amount contributed by the groom to the household expenses and usually paid after *katb il-kitab* (see below), while the *mu'akhkhar* is the amount the groom pledges to pay a) if he deserts her or divorces her; or b) in case of his death—this amount is immediately deducted from the inheritance and given to the widow before the rest of his assets are divided legally between the heirs.

With these arrangements completed, the engagement party is held. The fiancé presents his bride-to-be with the *shabka*, displayed on a velvet cushion for all the guests to admire. Normally the jewelry bought for the bride is in gold—encrusted with diamonds if the groom can afford it—and nowadays it has become a custom to buy a silver ring for the groom. The rings are worn on the right hand and the couple are now allowed to go out together, possibly unchaperoned, to get to know one another better.

The third step in the sequence of events is *katb il-kitab* (literally, 'the writing of the book'), which is the legalization of the bond or marriage contract. This is performed by the *ma'zun* (a sheikh holding a civil judicial post) either at home or in a mosque. The bride may or may not attend; if she does not she appoints a *wakil* (deputy)—usually her father, uncle, or any respectable male member of the family—to answer for her while she awaits the completion of the formalities in another room. The *ma'zun*, seated between the groom and bride or her deputy, solemnly asks the groom whether he accepts the young woman as his wife. On hearing an affirmative answer, he turns to the bride or her deputy with the same inquiry. If a deputy is officiating, and although he is well aware of his ward's response, he must go to her and officially ask her the same question. He then returns to the *ma'zun* and gives him her reply. The groom and bride, or deputy, then join their right hands, the *ma'zun* covers their hands with his, tops them with a white handkerchief, and all recite the *Fatiha*.

Recording all pertinent details concerning the couple—names, ages, positions, financial agreements, and so on—the *ma'zun* then asks two witnesses appointed by the families to corroborate the accuracy of the information recorded. The women seal the contract with a loud *zaghruta* (ululation), and the bride now joins the group. *Sharbat ward* (rose syrup) is offered to all present amid a chorus of *zagharit* (ululations), and the *ma'zun* takes his leave. The rings are now transferred to the third finger of the left hand, as it is believed that this finger is connected directly to the heart by the 'vein of love.'

The groom now offers his bride the *muqaddam* on a silver tray or in a box, to share in the expenses of the furniture and other household effects. Although they are now legally husband and wife, the couple do not actually live together until they make their wedding public by holding a reception. The reception may take place the day following *katb il-kitab*, or may be delayed any length of time—sometimes as much as a year or two—depending on the couple's situation and the completion of their home, and it is only at the wedding reception that the bride wears her white dress and veil.

Invitation cards giving the date and place of the wedding reception are delivered by hand at least a week before the event. Since today's homes cannot normally accommodate the number of guests invited (extended family, friends, and even business acquaintances), it has become fashionable nowadays to hold the reception in a hotel or 'club,' where dinner and a full entertainment program are provided. This reception is often a highly extravagant and expensive event, frequently breaking the bank for the parents. It has become more of a social obligation than a necessity, and most people endure the occasion mainly to follow the fashion.

Copts

Copts do not have a written code of matrimonial financial obligations, and individual families agree upon all these arrangements as their economic situation permits.

For their engagement, Copts hold a ceremony called the *Gabanyot* ('Our Father' in the Coptic language). This is held in their parish church, and is the occasion for the groom to present his bride with his gift of the *shabka*. The *Gabanyot* is an act constituting a preliminary contract of betrothal, binding both families ecclesiastically, but not judicially. All the financial arrangements agreed upon are recorded in the church register. In case of disagreement at a later date, this engagement can only be broken in church with the knowledge and consent of the parish priest, who will try his best to solve any problems leading to the rupture. Copts follow the same customs as Muslims in returning or keeping the presents if the engagement is broken.

Invitation cards announcing the church wedding must be hand-delivered to the guests by a member of the family at least a week before the event. Privileged guests also receive a card inviting them to attend the reception following the church wedding celebration.

Copts hold their wedding ceremony and reception on the same day. The wedding ceremony is always held in church in the afternoon or evening. The groom and male members of both families must arrive fifteen to thirty minutes earlier than the time stated on the invitation card to receive the guests. After exchanging handshakes, *mabruk* (congratulations), kisses, and greetings, the guests (who may be of both faiths) are invited to enter the church, which is decorated for the occasion. The guests must take their seats on either side of the church, as the middle aisle is cordoned off for the entrance of the bride and groom. Inevitably, the bride arrives at least ten minutes late in a noisy, boisterous procession of honking cars and *zagharit.*

The religious ceremony usually takes between twenty and thirty minutes, after which the couple move to the outer porch of the church. Here, surrounded by both sets of parents, they receive their guests' congratulations and kisses. (The legalization of the bond is made either the previous day by the couple, or on the following day by the officiating priest.) The couple then hurry to have their photographs taken, while the guests precede them to the place where the reception is to be held.

Muslims and Copts
At the door of the reception hall the guests are met by members of the families of the couple and invited to share a table with other

guests. Shortly after the time indicated on the invitation card, the blare of the _zaffa_ (announcement, or wedding march) is heard, heralding the arrival of the newlyweds.

The _zaffa_ is a joyous, raucous, and colorful procession, still enjoyed in its original form in villages and small towns, but modified in the capital and large cities to such an extent as to have lost its essential meaning. The _zaffa_ is the couple's announcement that they are now ready to live together. On the day agreed upon, the village bride, embellished and adorned with all her jewelry, rides to her new home in an open cart accompanied by her family, friends, and neighbors, all singing, clapping, and ululating to the accompaniment of a small band. Thus she arrives at her new home well 'announced.' In the capital and other big cities this procession has merely become the first part of the entertainment at the wedding reception.

The _zaffa_ may start at the top or at the foot of a main staircase and progresses upward or downward, depending on where the reception hall is located. Sometimes six or more bridesmaids, unmarried, wearing white dresses with a touch of pink, yellow, or blue, smiling sweetly and holding long candles adorned with ribbons and flowers, march on each side of the young couple. Small boys or girls with flower baskets hanging from their shoulders walk ahead of the couple, sprinkling their path with fistfuls of rose petals. Following the bride and groom come the parents, members of the family, and intimate friends, happily greeting and welcoming the guests, who flock on either side of the entrance hall to enjoy the procession. Usually a member of the immediate family is assigned to constantly and carefully arrange the bride's trailing veil.

At the head of the procession come the musicians—all men, who are also singers and dancers—dressed perhaps in white and red with gold strands. The band uses two types of instrument—trumpets, and *darabukka* and *riqq* (drum-like instruments). The music has a distinctive rhythm and is almost deafening in volume, as the musicians wear metal thimbles on their fingers to produce the loudest possible sound. They twirl, sing, and dance in successive solos or in a group, and are often accompanied by a belly dancer. The *zaffa* may take between thirty and ninety minutes, as the procession is made to stop at every few steps for a few minutes while the music, singing, and dancing continue. As they follow the procession, some members of the family, usually elderly members, toss *badra* (memento coins) bearing the couple's names over the heads of the guests. Many people will pick up a coin or two to keep as a souvenir, while small children inevitably dash under the guests' feet to fill their pockets with loot. Arriving at the reception hall, the procession then tours the hall, the couple exchanging smiles and greetings with their guests until they reach their *kosha* (two 'thrones' garlanded with flowers and raised on a platform to make the couple more visible). Here the entire troupe give their last performance and then retire, giving way to the rest of the entertainment and perhaps a sumptuous dinner.

Wedding guests generally come dressed to the nines—women bejeweled and wearing colorful dresses, and the men wearing suits or formal wear. Children, other than the immediate family, are not normally welcome at these receptions, and unless specifically asked, children should not accompany their parents.

Following the reception, which may last until the early hours of the morning, the newlyweds spend *laylt il-dukhla* ('the night of defloration'), their first night together, in the same city where their wedding reception is held. They will spend the night in a hotel or at a friend's apartment vacated for the occasion, but never in either parental home, as this would be considered a bad omen.

On the *sabahiya* (morning after the wedding) the parents and members of the immediate family pay a short visit to the newlyweds to wish them happiness, health, and prosperity, and to give them *nu'ut* (presents in the form of money). The couple receive their guests with a show of modesty, and the mother of the bride always manages to take her daughter aside for a quick tête-à-tête and to give her additional marital advice.

There is no specific time when wedding presents are sent to the newlyweds. Family members and close friends usually discuss with the young couple the nature of the gift they would like to receive— usually to complement their household effects. Colleagues at work often pool resources to buy the couple, again, something of their choice. In order not to embarrass them into a forced visit, colleagues usually ask the bride or groom when and where would it be convenient to send the present and he or she will indicate whether they would like the present to be brought to work, sent, or brought in per-

son—but it is more customary for the couple to receive their colleagues at home and proudly show them around their flat, delighted-
ly pointing out this or that piece of furniture or knickknack.

Divorce

Both faiths abhor divorce. For Muslims, a Hadith (a Saying of the
Prophet) declares, *al-Talaq abghad al-halal 'ind Allah* ('To God, the most
hateful of the permissible acts is divorce'), while the Bible says,
"Whosoever shall put away his wife, and marry another, committeth
adultery against her" (Mark 10:11). Yet divorce is not on the decline—
there are no definite statistics, but it seems that nowadays young married
couples are resorting to divorce more easily than earlier generations.

According to Shari'a law only the husband has the right to divorce
the wife, unless it is specifically stated in the marriage contract that the
wife is empowered with this right. This is called *al-'isma fi-idha* (the
right to divorce in her hand), but it is rare, as a husband usually feels
that allowing this right to his wife is an insult to his manhood.

In Islam, a husband has only to utter the three words, "I divorce
you," in her presence or absence, for the woman to find herself
divorced. However, if they wish to remarry, a divorced couple can do
so easily if the husband has divorced his wife once or twice only. If he
divorces her three separate times, however, or even utters the words
Inti tali' bi-l-talata ('You are thrice divorced'), the matter becomes more
complicated. The couple cannot remarry before she takes another
husband, called the *muhallil* (one who makes it *halal*, or permissible),

and the marriage is actually consummated. If after that the *muhallil* divorces her, then she can remarry her ex-husband.

A law passed a few years ago, the *khul'* (disassociation) law, now gives the wife the full right to request divorce in court, on condition that she renounces all matrimonial financial rights.

A divorced Muslim woman cannot marry a stranger until three months—the *'idda* (required number)—have elapsed since her divorce. This condition was enforced for paternity reasons—in order to ascertain that she is not carrying a child by her former husband.

For Copts, divorce is becoming more complex and unattainable. It has always been subject to great difficulties and the church will not grant divorce to either husband or wife except under the strictest of measures. Copts can circumvent these difficulties by one of the spouses changing his or her sect (Greek Orthodox to Roman Orthodox, or the like)—the couple being now of different sects, church laws are no longer applicable, and they will be able to divorce under Shari'a (Islamic law).

Subu'

The *subu'* (seventh day) ceremony is one of the most popular Egyptian childbirth traditions. Its origin derives from the ancient Egyptians, who, because of the high death rate in newborn babies, only celebrated the baby's arrival a week after the birth, when it was clear the baby would live. These rituals are nowhere more clearly depicted than in the Temple of Hatshepsut on Luxor's West Bank. Modern Egyptians also celebrate the arrival of the baby on the seventh day, in the afternoon. It also gives the mother a chance to rest after delivery so she can share in and enjoy the celebrations. This is the time when the baby is given its name, if this has not previously been decided.

Choosing a name for the baby—if it is not to have that of its grandfather or grandmother—occasionally causes some controversy, which may be resolved by the 'candle tradition': The parents agree on three different names and label each on three equal-sized candles. The candles are placed on a large tray in a conspicuous place away from draft. The tray contains nuts and beans sprinkled with rosewater, and an earthenware jar—an *'ulla* (open-necked water-jar) if the infant is a girl, and—with obvious symbolism—a pitcher if the baby is a boy. The *'ulla* is adorned with as many gold trinkets as the family owns, and the pitcher is decorated with natural or artificial flowers. The nuts, beans, rosewater, flowers, and gold all symbolize the parents' wishes that the infant be endowed with abundance, sweetness of life, prosperity, and happiness. The three candles are all lit at the same time, and the child is given the name of the last candle to burn out.

Most Egyptians—Muslims, Copts, rich and poor—follow more or less the same pattern of ritual for the *subu'*. The concept of this tradition was to dispel evil spirits and please the angels of the house, who in turn will look after the infant and grant it a good, happy, and successful life.

On the eve of the *subu'* friends join members of the family in the various preparations for the ritual. Like the ancient Egyptians, who offered seven beads of porphyry to Isis on this occasion, Egyptians now mix salt with seven different seeds: wheat, oats, broad beans, rice, corn, barley, and fenugreek—the salt wards off the evil eye, while the seeds ward off hunger. These items are put aside for the procession. Coins, candy, nuts, and dried dates are also mixed and kept separately, to be tossed in the air at the end of the party. Small bags or paper cornets bearing the baby's name and date of birth are filled with dried dates, candy, nuts, and a small candle, to be given to the guests as a souvenir when they leave. A highly calorific drink, *mughat* (made of fenugreek, ghee, and crushed nuts), is offered to guests with cakes and savories. Nursing mothers are urged to drink this concoction daily, as it is believed to enrich their milk.

On the appointed day the parents invite family and friends, especially those with young children, to share in their celebration—though whether invited or not, it is open house for all those who wish to visit and participate.

The party begins at sunset with salt being sprinkled all around the house to ward off the evil eye. The mother, carrying the baby in her arms, leads a procession of children holding small lighted candles and singing a partly nonsense rhyme, *Hala'atak, bergalatak, hala' dahab fi widanatak* ('. . . a gold ring in your ear'). The procession goes into every room, throwing handfuls of pulses to feed the evil spirits lurking in the corners and dispel them.

The baby is then placed in a large *ghurbal* (wooden sieve) on the floor, often decorated with flowers to symbolize domesticity and purification (associated with the sifting of flour). The mother is made to step over it seven times, symbolizing her authority over the infant. This is followed by the gentle rocking of the *ghurbal* from side to side, while a member of the family pounds a *hon* (brass mortar) near its head. Both the rocking and the pounding are meant to immunize the child against the hustle and bustle of life and instill in it valor and courage against hardship.

After impressing the infant with these formidable qualities, it is now time to introduce it to the humorous side of life. The baby is lifted from the sieve and the grandmothers and older members of the family enter into a verbal sparring match, advising the baby with silly instructions such as "Obey your mother, not your father," or "Smile to your maternal grandmother and frown when you see your paternal grandmother."

The party ends with the children singing, *Ya rabb, rabbina, tikbar wi tib'a 'addina* ('Lord, our Lord—may you grow up to be as old as we are'), whereupon the *ghurbal* is filled with the mix of dried dates, nuts, coins, and candy—made up the previous evening—and the contents are tossed in the air over the children's heads, who scamper on hands and knees picking up and filling their small pockets with the loot.

The ideal present given to an infant is any gold trinket, which apart from being ornamental is considered the baby's first savings. However *nu'ut* (gifts of money) given to the parents to buy something useful for the baby are slowly becoming an accepted norm.

Death

The first practice observed in the middle and upper classes when an Egyptian dies is that the name of the deceased and the names of the immediate family and close relatives are published in the obituary pages of the national newspaper *al-Ahram*. The time and place of the funeral and evening condolences, as well as the telegram address are also given. Some obituaries will state *La 'aza li-l-sayyidat* ('Women need not attend'), and in this case only the immediate family and intimate friends will go to the home of the bereaved and keep the women company.

The women attending the funeral or evening condolences wear black, while the men are expected to wear dark colors. If one cannot attend the funeral—and this is an obligation to which great weight is given—it is customary and virtually imperative to send a telegram or to telephone to express condolences.

Egyptian corpses are always buried, never cremated, and the burial always takes place within twenty-four hours of the death to avoid decomposition of the body owing to the hot and humid weather. There is a saying that clearly spells out this custom: *Ikram il-mayit dafnuh* ('Honor the dead by burying them'). Burials take place before sunset, a ritual borrowed from the ancient Egyptians, who expected Ra, the Sun god, to bless the bodies of the dead before retiring for the day.

To accommodate the families of the deceased, mosques and churches make available a *dar al-munasabat* ('hall of occasions') in the late afternoons and early evenings, where callers of both sexes and both faiths go to offer their condolences. Copts receive their callers in one large room, while Muslims retain two different rooms for men and women. For Muslims, a sheikh is engaged to recite verses from the Quran, while for Christians a priest or elder will give a sermon, quoting parts of the Bible. Turkish coffee, usually sugarless, is the only beverage offered, and this may be accepted or refused without embarrassment. The appropriate time one spends in these halls varies. One may enter while the priest is praying or the sheikh is reciting verses from the Quran, but no one may leave while this is continuing.

If the families do not wish to reserve a *dar al-munasabat*, but receive callers at home, the same arrangement is maintained, that is, two rooms to accommodate men and women separately for Muslims and one room for all for Copts.

The common expression of condolence used is *il-Ba'iya fi hayatak* ('May the days s/he did not live be added to yours'), to which the answer is *Wi hayatak il-ba'ya* ('May your life continue').

Muslims

When a Muslim dies, the first procedure is to summon a *mighassil* or *mighassila* (male or female corpse-washer) to bathe, cut the fingernails, plug the orifices with cotton, and wrap the naked body in a *kafan* (a white, seamless shroud in silk, satin, or cotton, as appropriate to the social standing of the deceased). Two members of the family must attend these rituals. The body is then placed in the bier in one room, while family and visitors sob and lament in a separate room.

A funerary service is held in the mosque after the noon or afternoon prayers, when the bier is placed facing the *qibla* (the direction of Mecca). Only men attend these services, while the women remain at home. After prayers, four or six members of the family or friends shoulder-carry the bier to the waiting car, all the while chanting, *al-Dayim, ma dayim ghayr Allah* ('Only God is everlasting'). The car is usually parked a short distance from the mosque, and the family stand in line beside it to receive the condolences. The bier is then driven to the burial ground accompanied by the immediate family and close friends.

Most families own a *hosh* (burial court) for their dead, cared for by a *ghafir* (guard) and his family, who may live in the premises. There is a common burial ground called a *sadaqa* (gratuity) for those who do not own a family *hosh*.

The *hosh* is an edifice that usually comprises a comfortably furnished room on the ground floor, with a square building canopied by a cupola under which is an underground room to house the remains of the family members. This underground room is separated in the middle by a wall or vault to house the two sexes separately. Here the bodies are removed from the bier and placed wrapped in their shrouds on the shelf beside the other bodies.

Muslims observe another ritual every Thursday until *il-arba'in* (the 'forty,' on the fortieth day after the death). A *fiqi* (Quran reciter) is engaged to come to the house and recite the Quran during these mornings.

In earlier times, the ancient Egyptians spent forty days mummifying the bodies of their dead and making preparations for the afterlife before holding their burial ceremony. Egyptians nowadays maintain this tradition as *il-arba'in*. The date is published in the obituary pages of the newspaper to inform those people who might wish to attend, especially those who were not able to offer their condolences at the time of the death. The normal ritual during the *arba'in* is to visit the tomb, with the women carrying specially made *shu'af* (a type of wheat bread), *fitir*, and fruit to distribute to the *ghafir*, his family, and the beggars who throng to the cemetery knowing they will be well rewarded with food and money. These are given with the request that a prayer be said for the soul of the departed.

Copts

If the deceased is a woman, family members will wash the body with eau de cologne and dress it before placing it in the coffin, while in the case of a man, the washing and dressing of the corpse is done by the coffin bearers.

Coptic funerals are held in church and are invested with a somber character—solemn tolling of church bells, black clothes for the women, dark suits for the men. Friends and acquaintances may send a wreath to the church to be transported later to the cemetery with the coffin. Women and men of both faiths attend a church service, with the sexes separating at the door—women to the right and men to the left. The immediate family of the deceased—also separated according to sex—sits in the first row. The coffin, covered in crosses that are either encrusted or inlaid with brass, is carried to the church before a doleful cortege of clergy and mourners accompanied by the intonation of psalms, while the priest circles and blesses the coffin, swinging the censer of burnt incense. Following prayers, the priest gives a sermon enumerating the deceased's good deeds and thanking the congregation for attending the funeral. The coffin is then carried out to the hearse followed by the men, who file out to shake hands with the immediate male members of the family, while the women remain in church and offer their condolences to the female members who remain seated in their places.

The coffin is driven to the burial grounds by the immediate family and close relatives, with the officiating priest chanting the appropriate prayers. Most families have their own *maqbara* (grave) taken care of by a *ghafir* (guard) and his family who, again, may live in the burial ground. The type of grave varies depending on the status of the family. Some of these edifices comprise a well-furnished sitting-room on the ground-floor with stairs leading to a room below lined with the burial shelves, while others have only an underground room topped with a slab of marble and a cross. The coffins are placed on the shelves side by side, irrespective of sex. Common burial grounds, *sadaqa*, are available for those who do not own a *maqbara*.

Copts observe a ritual on the third day following the death called *il-talit* ('the third'). On this morning, the priest calls on the family for added prayers and blessings. The family must prepare a bunch of parsley (or any other green leafy vegetable), a jug of water, and some items of the deceased's clothing. The priest dons his soutane, blesses these items, and then dips the parsley in the blessed water and goes around the house sprinkling the rooms and corners, all the while intoning prayers to dispel the soul of the deceased and wishing it everlasting salvation. Following this ritual, the priest and all those present will take the noon-day meal together, to which the parsley and water are added. The clothes are then given to the poor.

For the *arba'in,* Copts hold a special church service, publishing the date and place of the service in the obituary pages of the press. Those attending are offered *qurban* (holy bread) as *rahma* ('mercy') for the dead.

Muslims and Copts

After the *arba'in* it is considered appropriate for certain members of the family (cousins, aunts, and so on) to discard the black mourning dress.

The *sanawiya* (first anniversary) is the final religious rite to be observed by both Muslims and Copts. Muslims will retain a *fiqi* at home to recite verses from the Quran, while Copts will attend mass in memory of the deceased. Friends and family call at home or telephone saying, *Ti'ish wi tiftikir* ('May you live and remember').

To respect the traditions of the mourners, it is expected that people who come at any point to offer their condolences should:

- Wear black or a dark outfit.
- Talk in whispers, or keep silent.
- Never leave while the sheikh is reciting the Quran or the priest is giving his sermon.

If desired, a wreath can be sent to a Coptic funeral—it is an appreciated gesture—but not to a Muslim funeral.

Superstition

Superstition and superstitious beliefs are so ingrained in the Egyptian way of thinking that they have become part and parcel of the national tradition and mode of life. Different sectors of society adhere to different superstitions, and to mock or discredit any of these convictions will cause great offence.

The most common superstitious belief is *hasad* (the evil eye), and envy is its chief source. Its effect is believed to be extremely potent, as is eloquently expressed in the saying *Lawla al-hasad ma mat ahad* ('Were it not for envy, no one would die'). Gold and silver amulets and charms bearing the words *Allah* ('God'), *Ma sha' Allah* ('As God wishes') written in beautiful calligraphy are worn by Muslim women and small children to dispel the evil eye. Other symbols and mascots include the eye of Horus (the ancient Egyptian god of life), *khamsa wi-khmesa* (an open palm with the five fingers spread out), and *kharaza zarqa* ('blue bead'), which are also believed to have a protective effect.

There is no clear-cut expression or instance that defines or induces the evil eye, but it is always feared that open or overwhelming admiration of a person or thing will educe a spell. Thus it is considered improper for a person to show great admiration by exclaiming "How beautiful!" or any similar statement of praise. The approved expression is *Ma sha' Allah*, which is clearly understood as a compliment and at the same time a plea for God's blessing. Copts will use a further expression, *Bism il-salib* or *Rabbina yibarik* ('God bless'). Another saying is *'Eeni 'alek barda* ('My eye is cold upon you') meaning, "I do not throw fiery glances of envy on you."

As a sign of thanks to God and to dispel evil spirits, tradesmen or shopkeepers will never fail to kiss the first money they receive during the day and then touch their foreheads with it. This is called an *istiftah* ('opener').

There are specific items that are considered very potent in dispelling evil spirits, the most common being salt and alum. Salt is sprinkled on the ground or added to any burning object, while alum is either worn as an amulet or burned. For example, when a child falls suddenly ill of an undiagnosed fever it is customary for the family to blame someone's envious admiration of the child. Burning coals with a stick of alum and sprinkled with salt and incense is sure to identify the culprit. As it burns the alum becomes distorted and the family will claim that it resembles this person or that—the culprit. To counteract this spell, the burnt alum—the clue that unraveled the mystery—is tied in a cloth and thrown far away, while elderly people will mumble, *'Een il-hasud fiha 'ud* ('May the eye of the envious be pierced with a stick').

Some superstitious rituals have a clear explanation, such as:

Filling a charm with sand and hanging it over the doorstep. Sand symbolizes abundance—it cannot be counted—therefore such an act is a wish that the household be endowed with prosperity.

Decorating the house with new shoots at the beginning of the year is also a wish for prosperity.

Breaking an *'ulla* on a guest's departure is a wish that this person will never return. The ancient Egyptians believed that when a pharaoh or a nobleman died, his soul remained in limbo until the earthenware jar containing his belongings was smashed, thus releasing his soul and setting it free to soar far away. The resemblance here is very clear.

A few superstitious beliefs that are quite common:

Wishing to protect her infant son from death, a woman whose former children died at birth or shortly thereafter will give her newborn son derogatory names and dress him as a girl, giving him a girl's nickname; others will dress the child as a sheikh or monk and still others will beg clothes for the baby from door to door, however well-to-do the family may be. These ruses are supposed to protect the infant, delude evil spirits, and keep them far away.

If a person finds a morsel of bread in the street, they will pick it up, kiss it, and place it in an elevated place for birds or stray dogs to eat. Bread is so very highly esteemed by Egyptians that to throw it away is considered sacrilegious and sure to bring great misfortune on the guilty person.

If a group of friends find themselves happy and laughing hilariously, they may fear that their merriment might be turned into disaster and will exclaim, *Allahuma yig'aluh khayr* ('May God make it advantageous'). Others will refrain from great merriment or gaiety on a Friday, fearing a calamity on Sunday.

Egyptian Etiquette

The customary greeting is a handshake. Once a relationship has developed, greetings are commonly expressed with a kiss on both cheeks and the handshake, men with men and women with women.

Don't be surprised to see men holding hands or locking arms in the street. Friendship between men is an important part of the culture, and the fact that they are physical with each other should not be construed to mean a form of homosexuality.

See your guests to the door and do not abandon them before the elevators close or before they turn around the stairs and are out of sight.

When an Egyptian offers something, particularly food, there is a little game that goes on. It is customary to refuse what is offered at first, and to reluctantly accept at the insistence of the host. So don't take "No" for an answer in the beginning, but coax the guest to kindly accept what is offered.

Never leave a slipper or shoe turned upside-down. It is also deemed very rude to sit with the soles of the feet showing.

Sitting cross-legged in front of elders or superiors is a sign of disrespect.

It is probably best not to discuss religion, with any person of whatever faith.

It is always appreciated and considered a sign of friendship to visit a sick person in hospital or at home if he or she has undergone an operation. Ask about visiting hours, and take a present of chocolates, flowers, or any item of perfumery.

If you receive a visitor in the office, whether a colleague or a business acquaintance, begin by inquiring about his or her health and offer a drink—coffee, tea, or a soft drink in summer, coffee, tea, or cinnamon in winter—before broaching the subject of the visit. To ask a person immediately, "What can I do for you?" without the above preliminaries is considered abrupt and distant and may have a frosty outcome.

Following Sunday service in the Coptic Orthodox church, and on their way out, the congregation is offered *qurban* (consecrated bread). This bread is taken home or to the office or club, and morsels of it are offered to those not lucky enough to have attended the church service. If you do not want to eat it, do not refuse or throw it away—this is considered sacrilegious—but discreetly give it to another person, or place it in a conspicuous place for the birds to eat.

If there is a death in the building all the tenants should respect the occasion for the first three days, offering whatever help may be required by the family of the bereaved. The neighbors' television and radio volume should be lowered, and children should refrain from making too much noise or running up and down stairs.

Women should dress modestly when strolling in the street or shopping in town. Shorts are tolerated only in sports clubs or on the beach, never in the street.

Food

To most Egyptians, food is more than a necessity. It is a way of life, thought, and conduct. All social gatherings, from picnics to ceremonies and festivities, are an excuse to luxuriate in food. Very few people restrict their food intake to a well-balanced, healthy diet. Calorie-counting is almost completely ignored and indulgence in food is the norm—only when necessary will Egyptians go on a strict diet.

Fuul (beans) is the staple food of the average Egyptian. The most common dishes are *fuul midammis* (stewed beans) and *ta'miya* (bean cakes). *Fuul* is either scooped up in morsels of bread or sandwiched in *'esh baladi* (local bread), while *ta'miya* is eaten either accompanied by or sandwiched in *'esh baladi*.

Egyptians have a great respect for bread, bordering on reverence. The word *'esh* comes from *'esha* ('life'), which is quite understandable as— apart from its supply of carbohydrates—seventy percent of the protein intake of the average Egyptian comes from bread. It is considered *haram* ('sinful') to throw away bread, however small the morsel, as it is *ni'mit rab-bina* ('God's gift'). A passerby finding a piece of bread in the street will pick it up, touch it to his lips and forehead, then place it in an elevated place to avoid its being accidentally trampled on. Feeding stale bread to birds and pets is the customary thing to do. Bread also denotes a bond between people: a common expression denoting this bond of friendship is *Akalna 'esh wi malh ma' ba'd* ('We shared bread and salt').

Egyptian women usually prepare their dishes with fresh, home-grown produce. Although vegetables are now available in frozen form or in cans, most families still prefer fresh produce, believing that it imparts a better flavor. Herbs are always bought fresh. It is also unheard of to use desiccated onions or garlic powder—onions and garlic being two basic ingredients in most main dishes—instead of the real thing. Onions are peeled, chopped, grated, or sliced by hand, and although they cause the eyes to water profusely this inconvenience is thought to be very beneficial for the eyes, as the tears wash away impurities. Garlic, when cooked whole (peeled and unbruised so as not to waste its volatile oils), assumes a sweet, nut-like flavor and does not leave an unpleasant odor on the breath.

Most spices are bought in their crude form. They are roasted, grated, or crushed when needed, as people allege that freshly roasted and ground spices have more flavor than those bought ready-made in jars.

Beverages are also prepared at home from plants and herbs. In summer the most common drinks are *karkadeh* (hibiscus), *tamr hindi* (tamarind), *'ir' sus* (licorice) and *kharrub* (carob), which are both cooling and healthy. In winter, drinks are prepared mostly from spices: *'irfa* (cinnamon), *ni'na'* (mint), *yansun* (aniseed), and *hilba* (fenugreek). They are warming, and again very healthy. All these drinks are believed to have medicinal effects, benefiting kidneys, blood pressure, the digestive system, and so on.

Shay (tea) and *'ahwa* (coffee) are also enjoyed profusely by Egyptians—tea more than coffee. Tea is savored any time of the day or night and at almost all events and occasions. Tea leaves are often used, but a tea bag may be placed in every individual glass (not a cup), thus allowing each person to choose how long to steep the bag. The color of the infusion is as important as its taste, hence the preference for a glass rather than a cup.

Coffee is quite popular during the day, but to a lesser degree in the afternoons and evenings, as it is believed to cause insomnia. Coffee is sold plain or flavored, and in different degrees of roasting, while decaffeinated coffee is available only in imported jars. The coffee is brewed in a special metal pot called a *kanaka,* and is made with four different appellations according to the amount of sugar added: *sada* ('plain,' i.e., no sugar), *'al-riha* ('just a whiff'), *mazbut* ('exact'), and *ziyada* ('extra').

Vegetables play a central role in Egyptian cuisine. They also play a role in Egyptian slang. *Kosa* (zucchini) denotes corruption, *bitingan* (eggplant) is insanity, *'ar'* (gourd or squash) is undeserved flattery, *khiyar wi fa'us* (two types of cucumber) refers to discrimination, while the *tamatim* or *'uta* (tomato) has assumed the epithet of *magnuna ya 'uta* ('crazy tomato'), owing to its fluctuating price.

In Egyptian cuisine, tomatoes are a must. They are pressed, strained, and cooked with fried onions until the juice thickens and their color darkens, then other vegetables are added. These dishes of cooked vegetables swimming in tomato juice are served on the side of a mound of cooked rice on individual plates, or scooped in morsels of *'esh baladi.*

In times past, women in the cities were confined to the home and its innumerable chores. To while away the time in a pleasant, convivial atmosphere, the womenfolk of the entire family (two to three generations living under the same roof) would join together in a social gathering to prepare elaborate and intricate dishes. Nowadays, society has undergone dramatic change and women have many more chores to attend to inside and outside the house. They have less time for innovation and recreation and far fewer hands to help, yet the dishes are still prepared with the same patience, dexterity, and pride. *Sun'idaya wi-hyat 'eenaya* ('Done with my two hands, I swear by my eyes') eloquently describes these proud feelings.

One of the most popular and elaborate dishes, enjoyed in almost all circumstances, is *mahshi* ('stuffed'—the word 'vegetables' being understood). Practically all homegrown vegetables are used in *mahshi*, whether round (such as tomatoes, eggplants, sweet peppers, zucchini), or leafy (cabbage or vine leaves). There is a vast variety of filling ingredients, but rice and onions are the basic ingredients in all *mahshi*, which on restaurant menus is sometimes referred to by its Turkish name, *dolma*.

The skills of coring, spreading, rolling, and stuffing are learned by watching elder relatives an endless number of times as they prepare different *mahshi* dishes. The vegetables must be emptied of pulp, while the leaves must be boiled and carefully spread before the stuffing is added—the smaller and thinner the *mahshi*, the more presentable and palatable it is.

The normal manner of setting the table, whether for the family meal or for guests, is to place all the food on the table immediately before the diners come to the table. This gives everyone the chance to see the entire spread and to enjoy whichever dish he or she wants to start and end with. There should always be bread on the table, as well as salt and pepper. Muslims will preface their meal with a single word, *Bismillah* ('In the name of God'), while Copts will say grace with a short prayer.

When guests are invited to a meal, the food is prepared at home, and very rarely bought ready-made. The effort and care the hostess exerts in the preparation of the meal is the most eloquent sign of her welcome and concern for her guests. Food must be abundant, and when the meal is over the serving dishes must still contain food, thus making sure that everyone was satisfied and no one was deprived of a second or third helping. During the meal, and as a sign of welcome and hospitality, the hostess may apologize for not providing a better meal—*Basalit il-muhibb kharuf* ('An onion to the beloved is like a sheep'), she might say, meaning, "Owing to our love for you, please accept our humble meal."

Apart from denoting generosity, this habit of preparing a lot of food is practical, not wasteful. Most of the cooked food, especially stews, tastes just as good if not better when reheated, so leftovers can be enjoyed later.

Food is rarely eaten alone. Its preparation and consumption are one of the binding ties that stabilize each family as its members gather round the table. "The shortest route to a man's heart is through his stomach" is an international saying. True, yet to the Egyptian head of a family, the apex of his day's work, the joy and reward of his day's toil is the unity of the family gathered around a steaming dish and a well-prepared meal.

Guests at Meals

When Egyptians invite a person to their home it is usually to share a meal. Since many Egyptians are in the habit of napping in the afternoons, the normal custom among the middle and upper classes is to invite guests in the evening, when unless the host explicitly specifies a time of arrival, they are expected around 8 pm in winter or 9 pm in summer. However, guests in the medical or legal professions, who keep late office hours, are excused for coming much later. It is not uncommon for dinner to start after 11 pm.

Guests are not expected to bring food with them when invited, but flowers, chocolates, or sweet pastries (or, if the hosts drink alcohol, a bottle of liquor) are appreciated on a first visit. On entry the women kiss, while the men shake hands. If the guests are not strangers they may be met with the expression *Wahashtuna* ('We've missed you'). The guests are normally introduced to all the family members, although these do not necessarily remain sitting with the guests during the entire visit. In some houses women and men will separate into different rooms upon arrival and before dinner. Drinks (whether alcoholic or non-alcoholic), nuts, and *mezze* (hors d'oeuvres) are served before dinner.

The concept of privacy differs in Egyptian culture from that in the west. The reception room is the place for guests, not the kitchen, closed doors, or hallways—these are private. But conversely, asking guests personal questions about their finances, how much this or that cost, or where it was bought, where he or she spent the weekend, and so forth should not be regarded as rude or inquisitive prattle, but as a form of conversation and as showing an interest in the guests' welfare.

Itfaddalu ('Please come to the table'), the hostess announces when dinner is served. There is no seating arrangement and everyone is invited to sit at his or her leisure. All the food—soup, vegetables, meats, starches, and salads—are placed on the table right from the start of the meal. All are invited to help themselves, and taking second helpings is considered a sincere compliment. However, as a sign of hospitality the hosts will invariably push more food on their guests, irrespective of protests. The fact that guests do not clear their plates is not frowned upon, although the hosts may still coax them to eat more. To please your hosts, come with a hearty appetite and congratulate the hostess on her culinary prowess. Asking for the recipe of certain dishes is very flattering and much appreciated.

At the end of the meal, guests may say *Sufra dayma* ('May your table always be bountiful'), an expression understood to mean "May this house be always open to receive guests in similar happy occasions," or *Dayman 'amir* ('May your house always be prosperous'), and the hosts may reply *Damit hayatak* ('May you live long'). Then they all move back to the living room where tea or coffee is offered.

The Arabic saying *il-Deif il-magnun yakul wi-y'um* ('The crazy guest eats and leaves') eloquently describes the unbecoming behavior of an immediate departure after dinner. The time for leaving is at least half an hour after the end of the meal, when the hosts will always say *Lissa badri* ('It's still early'), and the guests, smiling, will again thank their hosts and express their compliments for the food and the company.

Street Food

In the late afternoons on street corners, along the banks of the Nile and in public gardens, vendors with their attractive singsong calls can be heard inviting passersby to enjoy their commodities. And roving mobile kitchens on carts abound during the day. Some serve *fuul* in the morning, while others serve *kushari* and *kibda* in the afternoon. Though the aroma emanating from these carts can be very appetizing, those with sensitive stomachs may want to think twice before partaking.

The main dishes served in this way are:

Fuul: A large, round, brass pot of stewed beans is placed in the cart, and usually concealed so that only the narrow neck and a small part of the vessel can be seen. Displayed on the cart are bottles of linseed oil and cottonseed oil, lemon juice, and jars containing cumin, salt, and chili. The vendor mashes the beans with these items on a small metal plate, pours the mix into halves of round *'esh baladi*, and presents it as a sandwich to the customer, as breakfast or lunch.

Kushari: This popular rich carbohydrate and protein dish is usually served later in the day. The vendor will dish out lentils, rice, and pasta from the mounds in front of him, top the whole with tomato sauce and onions and present it to the customer on a metal plate. From one or two sides of the cart hang buckets of water to rinse the plates after each use.

Kibda: Carts selling fried slithers of liver with a hot tomato sauce or *tahina* and *'esh baladi* can be seen in most working-class districts. The vendor halves the bread, mashes the liver in the bread with the required sauce, and presents the sandwich to the customer with pickles on the side.

Tirmis: A picturesque sight is the *bayya' il-tirmis* (lupine seller). He can be seen standing in front of a wooden cart bearing mounds of these small, round, yellow bead-like seeds. In one corner of the cart he has an *'ulla* filled with tap water to spray over the lupine seeds every now and then to keep them moist, and in another corner an artistic display of small paper cornets to fill with seeds for sale. The buyer holds the seed between thumb and index finger, bites on the skin to release the edible seed, then discards the peel. These vendors may also sell *hilba mizarra'a* (fenugreek sprouts) and *fuul nabet* (sprouting beans), but in smaller quantities.

A Ramadan *misahharati* beating his drum to wake people for the pre-dawn *suhur* meal. *Photograph by John Samples/IBA Media.*

A *kunafa* chef preparing the popular sweet. *Photograph by Mohamed Allouba/IBA Media.*

Breaking the Ramadan fast at a *ma'idat al-Rahman,* a public 'table of the Merciful.' *Photograph by Mohsen Allam/IBA Media.*

Ramadan lanterns and dates sold at a street stall. *Photograph by Mohsen Allam/IBA Media.*

Crowds, cars, and balloons coming together in festive 'Id spirit. *Photograph by John Samples/IBA Media.*

Wall paintings on a house recording the occupants' return from the *Hajj*.
Photograph by Dana Smillie/IBA Media.

Picnickers celebrating the spring festival of *Shamm al-Nisim* in a public park. *Photograph by Mohamed El-Masry.*

Woven palm fronds made to mark Coptic Palm Sunday. *Photograph by Claudia Yvonne Wiens.*

Libb and *sudani:* A cart with roasted and salted *sudani* (peanuts) and *libb* (watermelon and pumpkin seeds) is another interesting sight. Teenagers and young lovers buy these in small paper bags and amble along chomping the salted peanuts and biting into the pips to release the seed inside and spitting the peel in the street. Watermelon pips are also enjoyed by Egyptians at all times and all ages at home, especially while they are lounging in front of the television.

Dura mashwiya: A sight typical of summer is grilled sweetcorn. The corn is shucked and roasted over a charcoal fire set in a small metal receptacle. The vendor enumerates the merits of the corn in a pleasant singsong to the line of young lovers patiently waiting and inhaling the aroma of the roasting corn. When the corn is ready, the vendor envelops it in the shucked shell and presents it to the buyer. In Egypt, corn is only eaten grilled, not boiled or otherwise.

Batata mashwiya: Roasted sweet potato also has an aroma that attracts passersby from a distance. The vendors and their carts, which are set with a small charcoal oven, can be seen roaming the streets mainly in working-class districts. When roasted, the sweet potatoes turn a golden yellow, and are savored whole in their skins, which acquire a caramelized taste.

'Ir' sus: Bayya' il-'ir' sus (the licorice juice seller) is another attractive sight. The juice, with a block of ice, is placed in a large round flask surrounded by drinking glasses and suspended from the shoulder of the vendor by a leather strap so that it rests on his paunch. In one hand he carries two metal plates that he clangs rhythmically to accompany his singsong *Adi il-'agab, hilw min khashab* ('This is the wonder! Sweets from wood!'). He serves the juice by tilting the flask from a distance into the glass, allowing plenty of air bubbles to form in a thick foam.

Rites and Festivities

Mulids

Mulids ('birthdays' or anniversaries) are celebrated by Copts and Muslims to honor special saints or holy men. The origin of these celebrations is pagan and dates back to ancient Egyptian traditions, which have broken through the time barrier. There is nothing in Islam, for instance, that encourages the elevation or remembrance of holy men, yet in Egypt almost every district in large cities or towns has its 'holy man' buried under a dome or a tree.

Christianity came to Egypt at the beginning of the first millennium and was adopted as the state religion in the fourth century, but pagan rituals were not obliterated. Then when Islam came to Egypt in the seventh century another merger took place, and again the pagan rituals were taken over—the mulids are a clear confirmation of this process.

The program of events at these celebrations is dictated by tradition, and not by any religious obligations. The highlight is the procession that tours the neighboring streets, when young men carry—in the

case of Copts—banners with the picture of the saint being fêted, or—
in the case of Muslims—banners bearing the words *Allahu akbar*
('God is greatest') in beautiful Arabic calligraphy. They parade through
the streets, followed by a horde of children, swaying and dancing to
the rhythm of the *dufuf* (drums).

A few days before the event, the whole area is decorated with banners, flags, and twinkling lights. *Siwan*s (large tents) are erected to house
small local bands, a stage for the dancing girls and dervishes, and comfortable divans and cushions for the elderly to lounge and enjoy a gur-
gling *shisha* (water pipe). Dense crowds of revelers and hangers-on
throng to the area to rejoice in the noisy and joyful entertainment of
music, swings, ferris-wheels, merry-go-rounds, the famous *'aragoz* (pup-
pet show) and—most importantly—food and drink.

The last night of the *mulid* is called *il-leila il-kibira* ('the big
night'), and the entertainment here is at its best—belly dancers, buf-
foons, jesters, lotteries, recitals, games, and much more. A mari-
onette musical called *il-Leila il-kibira* by the famous cartoonist, poet,
and painter Salah Jahin depicts this big night with its puppets, dancing, and singing, and all its color.

Since *mulid* means birthday, some parents view this occasion as a
time to give thanks for the birth of a long-awaited child and ask benediction for him or her. After prayers, they will slaughter a sacrificial
lamb, distribute its flesh among the poor, and spray its blood on their
doorstep and in front of their house to ward off evil spirits and give
the child a happy life.

Most towns have their own *mulid*s for their saints and holy men, celebrated more or less in the same manner. Described below are two *mulids* celebrated in Cairo, Mulid al-Nabi (Birthday of the Prophet, celebrated by Muslims) and Mulid al-'Adra (Anniversary of the Virgin, celebrated by Christians).

Mulid al-Nabi is celebrated on 12 Rabi' al-Awwal (the third month of the Islamic calendar). Activity is concentrated in Hussein Square, where the procession is held, with chanting, swaying, and children running behind trying to imitate the elders. *Siwan*s are set up for the occasion, decorated with paper lanterns. Until the government banned them for health reasons, the streets were filled with bright stalls selling sweets in the form of dolls and sugar knights on horseback. The dolls stood, arms akimbo, in a flared dress and bright headdress of multi-colored paper, with painted black eyes and brows, red cheeks and lips. Often, the dolls and knights were not eaten, but stood in glory in the homes until the ants got them or they crumbled into decay. Nowadays there are plastic alternatives. In the tents, singers and satirists entertain the crowds all through the night until the muezzin's call to dawn prayer.

Mulid al-'Adra is celebrated on 21 August in Matariya, a
suburb of Cairo. The celebrations take place
around the Chapel of Matariya, which is dedicat-
ed to the Virgin. The sycamore tree—known as
the Tree of Mary—stands in the garden of the
chapel and is believed to be the tree under which
the Holy Family rested during its flight from
Herod, and where Mary nursed the infant Jesus.
The legend is similar to that of the ancient
Egyptians, when Isis was supposed to have
nursed baby Horus under a sacred tree in nearby
Heliopolis. The procession tours the premises
with the statue of the Virgin shoulder-carried by
praying young men. Again the celebrations here
take the form of swings, merry-go-rounds, ferris
wheels, and plenty of food and drink.

Muslim Festivities

Ramadan

Ramadan, the ninth month of the Islamic lunar calendar, is considered
the holiest month of the year. It is observed throughout the Islamic
world as a month of daytime fasting. Only the very young and the very
old, the sick, people on extended journeys, and menstruating, preg-
nant, and nursing women are exempt from fasting. Even if only one

person in the household is fasting, the entire family maintains a Ramadan schedule.

In accordance with one of the Five Pillars of Islam (see page 8), complete abstinence from food, drink, smoking, impure thoughts, and sexual intercourse must be observed from sunrise to sunset. If the faithful are unable to fast during this month, they are expected to fast extra days after Ramadan to compensate for any missed days.

The month starts on the evening of the last day of the month of Sha'ban with the *ru'ya* ('sighting'), when the new crescent moon is sighted with the naked eye. Ramadan lasts either twenty-nine or thirty days, ending with the celebration of the 'Id al-Fitr.

The end of the day's fast is announced by the sunset call to prayer from the mosques. In Cairo, a cannon is fired from the Citadel just before the prayer. After invoking God's name with the words *Bismillah*, the faithful enjoy *iftar* (breakfast)—very often a huge meal in a large joyful, family gathering.

As the faithful abstain from food for a long period of time—sometimes more than twelve hours—a special menu must be prepared that is not digested too quickly and keeps people feeling full for longer.

The first course is usually a thin, hot soup, believed necessary to prepare the stomach for the oncoming dishes. The main course might consist of *fuul* (beans) or meat dishes with the addition of pungent pickles to induce the diners to drink plenty of water. Vegetables and starches are also present. *Karkadeh* (hibiscus), *tamr hindi* (tamarind), and *'amar il-din* (apricot syrup) drinks are served lavishly to wash down this copious meal.

To rebuild the sugar level in the blood and revitalize energy lost through fasting, dessert always consists of very sweet dishes, the most common being oriental sweets, particularly *kunafa*, *'atayif*, and *khushaf*. People then leave the table to relax with some pleasant, quiet chitchat, or in front of the television, drinking endless glasses of sweet tea and nibbling *yamish* (dried fruit and nuts).

The other meal enjoyed during Ramadan is *suhur* (the daybreak meal). This meal is eaten anytime in the night before the muezzin's call to dawn prayers, and in the early hours a common sound is the rhythmic drumming and call of the *misahharati*, as he patrols the streets and alleys waking the people to take their *suhur*: *Is-ha ya nayim, wahhid il-Dayim* ('Wake up, sleeping one, and proclaim the unity of the Everlasting One'). *Suhur* is often a light meal, consisting of yoghurt, fruit, cottage cheese, or perhaps *fuul* and eggs. A few glasses of plain water are recommended at the end of *suhur* to fill the body's requirement and prevent it from later dehydration—especially in the hot summer.

Guests invited to *iftar* should arrive five to ten minutes before the sunset prayer to allow their hosts time to finish the last-minute preparations of the meal and to welcome them before ushering them to the table. Alcoholic drinks are not offered during Ramadan, even if the hosts indulge during the rest of the year.

A sight during Ramadan that is not seen at any other time of the year is the *ma'idat al-Rahman* ('table of the Merciful'), when a large number of tables and benches are placed on sidewalks, outside mosques, or in public gardens to feed the poor and homeless. These meals are donated by the wealthy and philanthropic every evening during the entire month as alms—an amazing and impressive logistical and charitable feat. Anyone and everyone is welcome to join without invitation.

A couple of hours after breaking their fast, some of the faithful go to the mosque for additional prayers called *tarawih*, which usually last an hour or two.

On 27 Ramadan, Muslims celebrate *Laylat al-Qadr* ('the Night of Destiny'), commemorating the night the Prophet received the first revelation of the Quran. It is believed that God answers prayers on this night.

Nightlife during Ramadan is very active, noisy, and joyful. Friends and neighbors exchange visits, shops open until well after midnight, crowds throng the streets, and children wearing bright clothes run to the street dangling their small multi-colored *fawanis* (lanterns, sing. *fanus*) and singing, *Wahawi ya wahawi, iyuha*—the words, unknown to most people, are in the ancient Coptic language and mean 'Welcome, welcome, moon,' referring to the new crescent of Ramadan. Old men sit in their regular coffee houses drinking mint tea and enjoying their *shisha*, while happily watching the hustle and bustle in the street. Large tents, *siwan*s, are erected in open spaces to accommodate various entertainment activities: one *siwan* frequented by literary circles will present a number of poets besting one another with their impromptu poems, others will have Quran reciters, and still others singers and entertainers. It is all a fantastic riot of noise, music, entertainment, and of course food—a haven for the sturdy and crowd-tolerant.

Some coffee houses offer a relatively recent activity during Ramadan—watching television. Apart from their usual clientele, who normally come to drink tea and play backgammon or dominoes, new patrons come to watch the special television serials and quizzes. The seating accommodations are rearranged in rows to accommodate the clients, who sit with eyes glued to the small screen, earnestly watching the quizzes and debating the solutions and results in the hope of winning one of the advertised prizes.

Since people do not get much sleep during Ramadan, some tend to get a little cranky during the day, especially when Ramadan falls during the summer with its high temperatures and long hours of daylight. To appease a quarrelsome person, one may say, *Ramadan karim* ('Ramadan is generous'), to which the reply is *Allahu akram* ('God is more generous'), expressions that usually bring the desired result of cooling tempers down.

During Ramadan, business and schooling come almost to a standstill during the day, starting late and ending early. Stores are laden with special provisions, especially nuts and sweets in anticipation of the nightly feasts. Most restaurants close during the day, except for those in the large hotels. Alcohol is removed from the shelves of stores and people carrying an Egyptian passport (of whatever faith) will not be served alcohol in any hotel or restaurant, day or night.

As a sign of respect it is advisable for everyone—foreigners, non-Muslims, and non-fasting people—to abstain from eating, drinking, or smoking in public during daylight hours in Ramadan.

'Id al-Fitr

'Id al-Fitr ('The Feast of Breaking the Fast') marks the end of the fasting period of Ramadan. This very joyful feast starts at the crack of dawn, when men gather at the mosque to pray, chanting *takbirat* (melodious litanies glorifying God).

After a sumptuous breakfast, the elders exchange visits and receive their friends who come to wish them a happy feast and are offered *kahk* and *ghurayyiba*, two traditional cookies eaten and offered to guests on this occasion. The greeting is *Kull sana wi-ntu tayyibin* ('May you be well every year'). For children, the 'Id affords many pleasures: the *'idiya* (money for the 'Id) given them by their elders, the new clothes, the swings and merry-go-rounds installed at street corners, and riding bicycles with spokes decorated with paper in clashing colors, all the while ringing their tinny bells for the simple pleasure of creating a racket. A couple of days before the 'Id, the children buy their supply of 'bombs'—small, round, brown-paper balls enveloping tiny pebbles and gun powder—which when forcefully thrown explode with a deafening bang.

The 'Id holiday lasts for three days. The first day is normally spent at home, but the following two days are often spent picnicking in public gardens, in the area around the Pyramids, or at the zoo. A look at the refuse littering these places at the end of the day vividly demonstrates the fun and the huge meals devoured outdoors.

The dead are not forgotten during feast days, as many women opt to go to the cemetery at this time to visit their dead, carrying the traditional pastries and sweet basil.

'Id al-Adha

'Id al-Adha ('Feast of the Sacrifice') takes place on 10 Dhu-l-Hijja, the
last month of the Islamic lunar calendar. It commemorates Abraham's
willingness to slaughter his own son Ismail in answer to God's com-
mand. However, the Archangel Gabriel intervened at the last minute
and replaced Ismail with a sheep, hence the tradition of slaughtering a
sheep.

This is also the time when Muslims (those who can afford it and
whose health permits) go to Mecca for the *hajj* (pilgrimage) to fulfill
the fourth Pillar of Islam (see page 9). The ritual of pilgrimage ends
on the morning of 'Id al-Adha.

To perform the pilgrimage Muslims wear the *ihram* (two pieces of
white seamless material devoid of any ornament, one around the waist
and the other thrown over the shoulders). A woman cannot go on pilgrimage alone, but must be accompanied by her husband or a *mihrim*
(a male relative such as an uncle, brother, or grandfather—whom it is
haram for her to marry) to perform this duty. Upon their return from
pilgrimage, the faithful proudly make their exalted position known to
one and all by driving around the streets with small white flags decorating their cars, and are henceforth known as *Hagg* or *Hagga*.

In small towns and villages, pilgrims decorate the outer walls of
their homes with paintings of the *Ka'ba* (the shrine at Mecca) or a
boat, plane, or camel to show how they traveled. This is not a religious
rite, but may derive from the practice of the ancient Egyptians, who,
following their pilgrimage to the temple of Osiris, God of the

Underworld, painted pictures of their journey on the walls of their tombs.

During the weeks before the 'Id, vendors trailing flocks of sheep come into the towns and cities to sell them to the faithful. These are usually bought a few days in advance of the Feast, to be fed and fattened for the occasion, and are left tethered to the iron railings of balconies, on roofs, or in gardens, where they are heard bleating day and night.

At dawn, repeated chants from the minarets are heard: *Allahu akbar, la ilaha illa Allah* ('God is great, there is no god but God'), and the early morning prayer is performed in the mosque or in a large square, where mats are spread beforehand for this purpose.

Immediately after morning prayers, the *gazzar* (butcher), guided by the bleating of the sheep, roams the streets, crying out *Gazzaaaar!* to let people know that his services are available. Invoking God's name, the butcher slaughters the sheep with a single knife stroke across the jugular, attended by a large audience of owners, neighbors, and friends. According to Islamic law, the sacrificial beast must be divided into three parts: a third is cut into small parcels and distributed among the poor, another third is given to relatives and neighbors, and the rest is enjoyed by the family, while the butcher walks off with his dues and the sheep's hide, which makes a thick rug that he sells or keeps for his family.

The 'Id al-Adha breakfast is unique. Unlike other days, when beans, eggs, and cheese are served, on this particular day breakfast consists of fried liver, fried kidneys, grilled meat, and so on, all washed down with glasses of sweet mint tea.

As on other festive days, all the family and friends gather to celebrate the 'Id together. The menfolk may stay at home to receive their friends and acquaintances who come to wish them a happy 'Id with the greeting *Kull sana wi-ntu tayyibin* ('May you be well every year'). Those who cannot come in person will telephone their good wishes. Meanwhile the women busy themselves with preparations for the midday meal. The usual foods to adorn the center of the table are *fatta* (bread and rice soaked in broth), *ru'a'* (puff pastry with ground beef), and other meat dishes to complement the buffet.

As at 'Id al-Fitr, children take their *'idiya* (money for the feast), don their new clothes, and go into the street to play on the swings and merry-go-rounds, ride their bicycles recklessly among the cars, or wage wars with their cap-bombs. Their delight reaches a height when they hurl a 'bomb' on the ground beside an unsuspecting passerby.

The 'Id lasts for a further three days, which people spend vacationing as they see fit—perhaps by the sea, by the Nile, or in the countryside.

Coptic Festivities

Coptic Fasting

The concept of Coptic fasting is the mortification of the body and soul from every indulgence and pleasure through physical hardship, that is, deprivation of vital needs—certain comestibles (food) and desires (sex). During fasting periods, the faithful must abstain from eating animal protein—meat and its byproducts, such as dairy products, although seafood is permissible at certain fasts—and sexual relations.

Unlike Islamic fasting, which is single in form and duration, Coptic fasting takes various forms and covers various periods. Some fasts last for three days, others for fifteen, and still others may extend up to fifty-nine days, occasionally bringing the total of fasting days in a year to 268.

The essence of the Coptic fast is in the type of food one is prohibited from ingesting, namely animal products. Thus the food eaten during these fasting periods is mostly vegetarian and non-dairy. However, to enliven the diet, many bakeries have instituted a new method of preparing all types of sweets and some foods with hydrogenated oil in place of butter.

The Coptic Church has never specified the age limit at which children should start fasting. This is left to the discretion of the parents and parish priest, who often encourage children to fast from the young age of eight or ten. Fasting at an early age is considered a sign of devotion.

With very few exceptions—the fast before Christmas, the fast of the Virgin, and fasting on Wednesdays and Fridays—the fasts do not have fixed dates but vary every year according to the date fixed for the Coptic Easter. The Coptic fasts of the year are as follows:

Wednesdays and Fridays of almost every week of the year:
Wednesdays in memory of the plot against Christ
and Fridays in memory of his death. On these two

days Copts must abstain from meat and dairy products, but are allowed to eat seafood. For the fifty-five days following Easter the faithful are not subject to this fast.

al-Siyam al-Saghir ('the Small Fast') starts on 25 November and lasts for 43 days until Coptic Christmas on 7 January. The first three days are observed to commemorate *intiqal al-gabal* ('the moving of the mountain'), a story dating back to the twelfth century, during the rule of the Fatimids. The then ruler had threatened to persecute the Copts as heathens unless they showed him a sign from heaven proving the veracity of their faith by moving the Muqattam Mountain. Headed by Simaan al-Kharraz (Simon the Cobbler), the Copts fasted and prayed for three days, at the end of which the mountain was hit by an earthquake and actually moved. The ruler was so awed and troubled by this event that he allowed them to pursue their faith. In memory of this miracle, Copts refrain completely from partaking of any food until evening prayers, as their predecessors did. The following forty days are observed in memory of the forty days the Jews fasted in Sinai before Moses received the Word of God and the Ten Commandments. During this fast seafood is permissible in the daily menu.

For *Siyam Yunis* ('the Fast of Jonah'), who was swallowed by
the whale for three days, Copts fast for the same
period of time by abstaining from food and drink
completely until evening prayers, after which they
will eat only vegetables and fruit. This fast comes
two weeks before Lent.

al-Siyam al-Kabir ('the Great Fast,' or Lent) lasts for fifty-five
days—the traditional forty days that Christ fasted on
the Mount of Olives, plus a week before (the reasons given for this week of fasting vary) and a week
after, as penance for Holy Week. As Easter is not a
fixed date, neither is Lent or the Fast of Jonah.
After Easter, there is a respite of fifty-five days
without fasting, Wednesdays and Fridays included.

Next comes *Siyam al-Rusul* ('the Fast of the Apostles'), whose
timing and duration are variable. It must start immediately after the elapse of the fifty-five days and end
on 12 July, when Copts celebrate 'Id al-Rusul ('Feast
of the Apostles') in memory of the deaths of St.
Peter and St. Paul. This fast may last for fifteen to
fifty-nine days depending on the date of Easter.

Siyam al-'Adra ('the Fast of the Virgin') is observed from 7 to
21 August. During this period, abstinence from fish
is left to the pope's discretion. Whereas the former
pope, Kirollos VI, allowed the congregation to eat

seafood, the present patriarch, Shenouda III, added
fish to the list of prohibited foods.

Among the many books about Coptic fasting, two clarify the rea-
soning behind the concept. The first, *The Spiritualism of Fasting* by
Pope Shenouda III, outlines the benefits and merits of vegetables.
Comparing vegetables with meat, the pope emphasizes their advan-
tages, claiming they are light on the digestion and soothing, whereas meat, or animal protein, is saturated with fat and is therefore
heavy to digest and harmful to the health. He also mentions that
this theory is not contrary to our eating habits: we eat only herbiv-
orous animals, not carnivores, as the former are mild and tame,
unlike the latter, which are wild, ferocious, and inedible. To promote
the benefits of vegetables, he points out that far from weakening
the body, vegetables give it strength and vigor. He gives as examples
of healthy vegetarians Adam and Eve—Adam is supposed to have
lived for 930 years—and George Bernard Shaw, who lived for 94
years; and in the animal kingdom the bull, the camel, and the
horse—all herbivores that mature into strong animals. The pope
also enumerates several examples of hermits, saints, and pious men
who all purified their souls through fasting, either by abstaining
from all types of food for long periods of time, or simply by
abstaining from animal protein. As a further sign of devotion, he
encourages the faithful individual to add a food he or she particularly likes to the list of forbidden items.

The second book is *The Christian Fast: Sacrificial Love,* by Father Youssef Assaad. Father Assaad elaborates in clear terms why Copts must abstain from sexual relations during their fast. He explains that fasting is not only abstinence from food and drink but also deprivation of all physical desires and passions, such as sexual intercourse. Since the animals we eat (herbivores) procreate through intercourse, their flesh will naturally be infused with this instinct and will automatically impart it to those eating their meat, which is against the concept of abstention. Fish on the other hand, lack this instinct, as fish eggs are fertilized outside the body, and this is why fish is allowed in certain fasts. With this simple explanation, Father Assaad clarifies the reason behind the Church's prohibition against holding weddings during fasting periods.

Christmas

The Coptic Orthodox *'Id al-Milad* (Christmas) is celebrated on 7 January, and is now an official national holiday in Egypt. In the Coptic calendar, it falls on 29 Kiyahk, and is preceded by forty-three days of fasting (see above). Abstinence from animal protein and its derivatives is the rule, but seafood is allowed.

A few days before Christmas day it is customary for families to place various pulses (beans, lupines, lentils, chickpeas, and so on) on separate small plates lined with wet cotton and left to germinate in a shaded, secluded place. The small shoots are then placed all around the home as decoration and as a wish for *sana khadra* ('a green year')—that is, for prosperity and fertility.

In the early evening of 6 January, at around 8 or 9 pm, the faithful go to church to attend a mass that usually ends before midnight, after which they go home to a very meaty meal to end their long fast. The traditional dishes are *fatta*, *mumbar* (chitterlings), and any other meaty dish, and usually an assortment of *mahshi* (stuffed vegetables).

On Christmas morning families exchange visits and receive guests who come to wish them a happy feast, using the same greeting as the Muslims on their feasts: *Kull sana wi-ntu tayyibin* ('May you be well every year'). Visitors are offered *kahk* and *ghurayyiba* pastries. Friends who are unable to come in person telephone with their good wishes.

Balloons showing Father Christmas and the Christmas tree are slowly gaining their place among the well-to-do, but not the western tradition of exchanging gifts. Only the older members of the family are in the habit of giving children an *'idiya* (money for the feast).

Epiphany

'Id al-Ghutas ('the Feast of Immersion'), or Epiphany, is celebrated on 19 January. This festival marks the end of the Christmas season and commemorates the baptism of Christ. For their baptism, Copts immerse the entire body of the child in the font three times, hence the name *Ghutas*.

On this particular day, Copts eat *'ul'as* (colocasia or taro) cooked as a stew. A popular saying, reflecting the importance of eating colocasia on this day, asserts: *Law makaltish 'ul'as, tisbah bidun ras* ('If you don't eat colocasia, you will wake up without a head'). And folklore has it that on this particular day rain must fall to wash the cooking pots.

Children have their own festive ritual for celebrating *Ghutas:* tangerines, which abound during this season, are emptied very carefully by making two small triangular slits in the upper half of the peel, which leaves the tangerine shaped like a basket; a small candle or wick dipped in oil is placed inside the basket and lighted to adorn the table at the midday meal.

Holy Week and Easter

During Holy Week, church services are held daily from morning until early afternoon.

Hadd al-Za'f (Palm Sunday) commemorates the entry of Jesus into Jerusalem riding a donkey. Although this is a celebration, Copts do not cease their fast but continue their abstinence from animal protein until Easter.

On the eve of Palm Sunday, children skillfully plait crosses and donkeys from palm fronds, which they take to church on the following day. Mass is a joyful event, with a procession of children chanting psalms and holding lit candles and their palm figurines touring the church. The priest blesses the figurines, which the families then hang on their front doors.

Khamis al-'Ahd ('Covenant Thursday,' Maundy Thursday) commemorates the Last Supper. At the end of church service, the priest dips a handkerchief in water that he has blessed and wipes the foreheads of his parishioners, in lieu of symbolically washing their feet.

al-Gum'a al-Hazina ('Sad Friday,' Good Friday) commemorates the death of Christ on the cross. Copts abstain from food and drink from sunrise to sunset and attend services in church in the afternoon. It is only after the end of services that they have their first meal of the day, which is traditionally *ta'miya* (fried bean cakes) and *fuul nabet* (sprouting beans), prepared at home. Almost every Coptic family has its own recipe for these two items.

'Id al-Qiyama ('the Feast of the Resurrection,' or Easter) ends the fifty-five days of fasting. On *Sabt al-Nur* ('Saturday of Light,' Holy Saturday) the faithful attend late mass at around 10 pm. After prayers the congregation congratulate one another in both Arabic and Coptic with *al-Masih qam / Christos anesti* ('Christ has risen')—to which the answer is *Haqqan qam / Anestos nesti* ('Truly he has risen')—they go home to indulge in their first taste of *zafar* (meat dishes) after almost two months of abstinence. This meal usually consists of the entrails of mutton—liver, kidney, and tripe.

On Easter morning, after a copious breakfast of eggs, cheese, and milk, the men go visiting or receive their friends, the children take their *'idiya* and run into the street in their new clothes to throw their 'bombs,' while the women busy themselves with preparations for the midday meal, usually enjoyed with an extended family. The traditional greeting for Easter is again *al-Masih qam* (with the response *Haqqan qam*), but of course one may also use the general greeting for any special occasion, whether Christian or Muslim: *Kull sana wi-ntu tayyibin* ('May you be well every year').

Feasts are always an occasion for families to enjoy a banquet. Meat dishes abound at the table at Easter, the most important being *fatta* and *wara' 'inab* (stuffed vine leaves). *Kufta*, a leg of lamb, and roasts might also be served on this festive day.

During the preceding week, *kahk* and *ghurayyiba* pastries are prepared to be enjoyed by the family and offered to the guests who come calling to wish the family a happy feast.

Secular Festivities

Shamm al-Nisim

Shamm al-Nisim ('Smelling the Breeze') is the oldest holiday in Egypt and has survived uninterrupted from ancient times. Egyptians have changed languages, religions, allegiances, and division into classes and factions, but this spring festival has remained alive through the ages and up to the present day.

Originally a pagan festival, *Shamm al-Nisim* is celebrated on the Monday following the Coptic Orthodox Easter, and is observed by all Egyptians—Copts and Muslims, rich and poor, young and old—and in the open air: in a public garden, around the Pyramids, along the Nile or, for the lucky few, at a private *'izba* (farm or estate).

On the eve of *Shamm al-Nisim*, preparations for the traditional morning meal commence. The most important items are green onions, *fisikh* (salted raw mullet), and hard-boiled eggs. In spite of the proliferation of synthetic dyes, most Egyptian homes prefer to color their eggs with onion peel, which imparts a light brown color; the eggs are then made shiny by rubbing them with a piece of cotton dipped in oil. The colored eggs are placed in a prominent place for all to see and admire before they are eaten.

The ritual starts early in the morning with the parents rubbing the sleepy children's noses with spring onions dipped in vinegar. The pungent smell tingles their nostrils and makes them jump out of bed, which is precisely the desired effect. Apart from making them alert and active, onions are also believed to give children immunity against disease.

The children don their colorful new clothes and run out to play. Handcarts bearing colored conical hats and musical horns made from cardboard for sale are found on many street corners. The children happily wear these hats and compete in blowing the horns, issuing very jarring, discordant notes.

Sailing boats bedecked with small, multicolored triangular flags fluttering in the breeze and loaded with families, the children noisily singing and playing drums, tambourines, and horns, cruise the Nile. In some public gardens, as well as on some side streets, metal swings and merry-go-rounds are installed, and bicycles with multicolored paper decorating the spokes are available for hire. The children ride these bicycles in and out of traffic, making as much noise as they can with their tin bells.

Licorice juice vendors, colorfully dressed for the occasion, clank their metal plates in a rhythmic beat to accompany a sing-song refrain enumerating the merits of their beverage. Lupine vendors displaying mounds of the attractive yellow seeds on hand-drawn carts fill small paper cornets with the pulses for people to enjoy. Fenugreek sprouts and sprouting beans are also on sale to the feasting crowds.

Although many Egyptians will seize the opportunity to spend the whole day out picnicking, the principal meal on *Shamm al-Nisim* is breakfast, which is taken as early as 6 am. The families gather in large groups—uncles, aunts, cousins, grandparents, and grandchildren—to join in the traditional breakfast of onions, eggs, and *fisikh*, accompanied with glasses of sweet mint tea. Lettuce, *malana* (baby chickpeas) and *fuul hirati* (green field beans) are enjoyed at the end of the meal: the pods are individually emptied and the beans savored as an aid to digestion.

Many myths explain the symbolism of the culinary items enjoyed at *Shamm al-Nisim*. Eggs have always symbolized new life, and coloring them is a wish that life to come will be happy and cheerful. Green onions come down from the ancient Egyptians, who believed that onions not only warded off evil spirits and the evil eye but also cured most diseases, while fisikh symbolizes preservation from hunger—the ancient Egyptians salted their fish to preserve it through the dry season. The leafy green plants—lettuce, *malana*, and *fuul hirati*— represent fertility.

Proverbs

EGYPTIANS PUNCTUATE THEIR day-to-day conversations with many proverbs. They have proverbs for almost every situation: mutual respect, fairness, obedience, modesty, generosity, accepting the status quo, and so on. These proverbs are used to stress an argument, prove or negate a situation, or simply because they are the fruits of Egypt's 'glorious past.'

Most of these proverbs are wise sayings and useful to know. Understanding the meaning behind proverbs will help outsiders empathize with the Egyptian way of thinking. Here are some of the most common proverbs, with their meanings and usage:

'Add lihafak, midd riglek ('Stretch your legs as far as the size of your quilt'). Live according to your means.

Khud ma 'atak, wi-truk ma fatak ('Take what is coming and leave what is past'). Don't look back.

il-Bab illi yigi minnu il-rih, siddu wi-starih ('The door that brings in the wind, close it and relax'). Avoid causes of friction.

Ma-yinob il-mukhalis illa ta'ti' il-hudum ('The mediator gains only
        torn clothes). Don't interfere, you lose out in the end.

Lamma yu'a' il-tor, tiktar il-sakakin ('When the bull falls, the
        knives grow in number'). Slander increases after the
        downfall of a person in power.

Kullu 'ind il-'arab sabun ('To the Arabs, it is all soap'). Everyone
        is equal.

In kan habibak 'asal matilhasush kullu ('If your friend is sweet as
        honey, don't lick him all up'). Don't take advantage
        of a dear friend.

Ma'idirsh 'ala-l-humar, yitshattar 'ala-l-barda'a ('He could not beat
        the donkey, so he beat the saddle'). Those who can-
        not triumph over the strong vanquish the weak.

Yiddi il-hala' li-lli bila widan ('He gives earrings to those without
        ears'). Some people acquire things they are not quali-
        fied to have.

'Ulna tor, alu ihlibuu ('We told them it was a bull, they said milk
        it'). Insistence on inaccessible things, or a descrip-
        tion of stubbornness.

Yimut il-zammar, wi suba'u biyil'ab ('The trumpet player dies and
        his finger is still playing'). Old habits die hard.

Sikitnalu, dakhal bi-humaru ('We accepted him, and he came in with
        his donkey'). Give him an inch, and he'll take a mile.

il-'Ilm fi-l-ras, mish fi-l-kurras ('Knowledge is in the head, not in the
        book'). Learn to think instead of amassing information.

Min tarak daru, 'all mi'daru ('Who leaves his home loses his
prestige') One's prestige is among one's own people.

il-Kidb malush riglen ('A lie has no legs'). Lies are always found
out.

Yisum, yisum, wi yiftar 'ala basala ('After fasting, he feasts on an
onion'). Expression of disappointment at an unex-
pectedly poor response.

il-'Irsh il-abyad yinfa' fi-l-yom il-iswid ('A white piaster will be
needed on a black day'). Every penny counts
towards a rainy day.

il-Markib illi fiha rayisen tighra' ('A boat with two captains will
sink'). Too many cooks spoil the broth.

Ma-yi'gibu il-'agab, wala-l-siyam fi-Ragab ('Nothing pleases him,
not even fasting during Ragab'). This is said of a
person who is difficult to please.

Illi-tlasa' min il-shurba yunfukh fi-l-zabadi ('He who is burned by the
soup blows on the yoghurt'). Once bitten, twice shy.

il-Ghayib luh 'uzru ('The absent person has his excuse'). Don't
jump to conclusions.

Illi fat mat ('What is past is dead'). No use crying over spilt milk.

Ba'd ma shab, wadduu il-kuttab ('After he grew old, they sent him to
primary school'). You can't teach an old dog new tricks.

Labbis il-busa, tib'a 'arusa ('Dress up a reed and it becomes a
doll'). Cosmetics can turn an ugly duckling into a
swan.

Itlamm il-mat'us 'ala khayib il-raga ('The miserable got together
        with the hopeless'). No good can come out of such
        a union.

il-'Ird fi-'een ummu ghazal ('The monkey is a gazelle in his moth-
        er's eyes'). When you are biased you see things
        through rose-colored glasses.

il-Rusasa illi matsibsh tidwish ('The bullet that does not hit its
        mark still makes a noise'). Even if an accusation
        doesn't stand, it still hurts.

il-'A'l zina ('Brains make a person look good'). Wisdom is
        beautiful, ignorance is ugly.

al-Tuyur 'ala ashkaliha taqa' ('Birds fall together according to
        their type'). Birds of a feather flock together.

Ya bakht min kan il-naqib khalu ('Lucky is the one whose uncle
        is a captain'). It helps to have relatives in high places.

Hiya-l-gilla asbahit karamilla? ('Did the dung turn to caramel?').
        Don't expect a bad person suddenly to turn good.

Ya hashir nafsak been il-basala wi-shrit-ha, ma-yinobak illa sannit-ha
        ('If you come between the onion and its peel all you
        will get is the bad smell'). Mind your own business.

Ibn il-wizz 'awwam ('The son of the goose is a good swimmer').
        Like father, like son.

Asma' kalamak asadda'ak, ashuf 'umurak astaghrab ('I believe
        what you say, but am surprised at what you do').
        You say one thing and do another.

Khud min il-tall, yikhtall ('Take from the hill, and it will fall
    down'). Every little counts.

Iddi il-'esh li-khabbazu ('Give the bread to its baker'). Give the
    job to the specialist.

Kul ma yi'gibak wi-lbis ma yi'gib il-nas ('Eat to please yourself, but
    dress to please others'). Said to a person who tries
    to be different.

Recipes

FOLLOWING ARE RECIPES for some of the foods and drinks mentioned in this book.

'Ahwa (coffee): Powdered Turkish coffee is bought unfla-
vored or flavored with cardamom and/or dried
powdered citrus peel. The ordinary sized coffee
cup holds about two ounces of liquid. Pour
water in a *kanaka* and place over fire. Add one
teaspoon of coffee and sugar (if required) and
remove from heat as soon as the mixture rises
and forms a layer of foam. Serve immediately,
making sure to shake the hand very gently while
pouring, to collect all the foam into the cups.
Served as: *sada* (sugarless); *'al-riha* (half a teaspoon of sugar); *mazbut* (equal amounts of coffee and sugar); or *ziyada* (two teaspoons of
sugar).

'Amar al-din (apricot syrup): Shred sheets of dried apricot and
dissolve in boiling water. When completely dis-
solved, add sugar, stir, and refrigerate.

'Ashura ('tenth'): Boil wheat, strain, then add enough sweetened milk with a few drops of rose water to make it
mushy. Top with raisins and crushed nuts.

'Atayif (sweet dumplings): Place filling—a mixture of crushed
nuts, cinnamon, and sugar—on half a circle of
'atayef and fold over, pressing down firmly with the
fingers. Deep fry or place on a baking tray, dabbing
each one with ghee or butter. When fried or baked,
saturate with cold sugar syrup.

Fatta: Layer pieces of hard bread and moisten with well-sea-
soned broth to which fried crushed garlic and vinegar have been added. Top with cooked rice and
again moisten the whole with broth. Cover with
boiled pieces of neck meat, or chicken.

Fisikh (salted raw mullet): Singe *fisikh* lightly over a naked
flame. The skin will shrivel; discard skin and back-
bone, flake, and marinate in lemon juice.

Fitir: Prepare dough and roll very thinly. Place small dabs of
butter on dough, fold over, and roll again. Shape
into 10 x 10 cm squares, 1 cm thick, and bake.

Fuul (beans): Beans are stewed and mashed with oil, lemon
juice, cumin, and salt. This is the basic breakfast

dish. You may add eggs and pickles, or the beans
may be cooked with sliced green peppers, thinly
sliced fried onions, roughly chopped tomatoes,
and salt and pepper, and moistened with oil; or
stewed, mashed, and cooked with savory minced
beef.

Fuul nabet (sprouting beans): Soak beans in an earthenware
container for four to six days, rinsing and changing
the water ever twelve hours. They are ready when
they have germinated and the sprouts are at least
one centimeter long. Boil with sliced onions, add
cumin, seasoning, crushed garlic, and lemon juice.
Cool and mix with fresh chopped parsley.

Ghurayyiba (a type of shortbread): Whisk one measure of ghee
thoroughly before adding slowly half a measure of
sugar and two measures of flour. Shape into small
rounds and bake in the oven. Press a sliver of almond
into the top immediately after they are removed from
the oven.

Hilba (fenugreek): Boil fenugreek seeds (one teaspoon of fenugreek to one cup of water) for fifteen minutes until
tender. Sweeten and serve in individual cups together
with the seeds.

Hilba mizarra'a (fenugreek sprouts): Place a thin layer of seeds in a
sieve over an empty pot and cover with a wet cloth so it

is kept damp until the fenugreek sprouts through the
holes of the sieve are about five to ten centimeters long.

'Irfa (cinnamon): Boil one cup of water with half a teaspoon of
cinnamon powder for one to two minutes until the
water absorbs the fragrance. Strain, sweeten to taste,
and serve, sprinkling crushed mixed nuts on each cup.

'Ir' sus (licorice): Place licorice powder in a deep bowl and cover
with cold water. Stir with a spoon until it forms a thick
paste. Allow to rest for twenty minutes, then place in a
cheesecloth bag, suspend in a jug filled with water, and
refrigerate. Before serving, squeeze the bag gently in
the jug, then discard bag and contents. Pour the juice
into individual glasses from a height, to allow plenty of
air bubbles to form a thick foam, an important feature
in drinking licorice juice.

Kahk: Dilute yeast in warm water. Sift flour with a pinch of salt,
mix with melted ghee and diluted yeast to form a ball
of dough, and leave to ferment at room temperature.
Prepare the filling by frying flour in ghee until it
assumes a yellowish color, remove from heat, mix thoroughly with honey, then return to the heat and cook
until it assumes a thin custard-like consistency called
'agamiya. Pierce the small ball of dough and insert a
small amount of *'agamiya*, then roll back and close the
dough in the shape of a dome. Bake in the oven. When

cooked, sprinkle generously with powdered sugar.

Karkadeh (hibiscus): Soak dried hibiscus sepals in water, filter and sweeten to taste. Can be drunk ice-cold or hot. Or soak in water, then boil and filter—the leaves can be used in several boilings to make a larger quantity. Sweeten to taste and drink hot or chill before serving.

Kharrub (carob): Boil powdered carob for two to three minutes, filter, sweeten to taste, and then refrigerate.

Khushaf (dried fruit compote): Parboil dried apricots, figs, prunes, dates, and raisins. Do not discard the water, but when cool add nuts—almonds, hazelnuts, and/or walnuts—and a drop of rose water, then chill before serving.

Kibda (liver): Cut thinly, season, and fry with thinly sliced onions.

Kufta: Mince beef and onions twice or pound to a smooth consistency. Soak bread in milk or water, drain, then add to meat with seasoning. Mix well and shape into either rounds or fingers. Serve either fried or grilled.

Kunafa (noodle pastry): Mix with butter, then spread a thick layer of *kunafa* on a baking tray, add a mixture of crushed nuts, cinnamon, and sugar or sweet white sauce, cover with another thin layer of *kunafa* and bake in the oven. When cooked, remove from the oven and saturate with cold sugar syrup.

Kushari: Boil brown lentils, rice, and macaroni separately in salted water, then place all together in a pot. Fry onions to a rich brown color, strain, place on absorbent paper and add the oil to the lentil mixture. Prepare tomato sauce (with optional hot chili) and serve, topping each plate with tomato sauce and fried onions. It is interesting to note that although *kushari* is a very popular Egyptian meal, its origin is an Indian dish called *khichri*, which is also the origin of English kedgeree.

Mughat: Fry powdered fenugreek in ghee and add to sweetened water, then place over the heat to boil until it thickens to the consistency of custard. Serve hot or cold, sprinkling each individual cup with crushed nuts.

Mumbar (chitterlings): Prepare stuffing (rice, finely chopped onions, ground beef, and seasoning), tie one end of the chitterling and fill loosely with the stuffing. Shape like a sausage, tying thread every ten centimeters or so. Boil with cardamom seeds, mastic, and seasoning. When cooked, remove from the broth, fry, discard the thread, cut at intersections, and serve.

Ni'na' (mint): Bring one cup of water to the boil, add half a teaspoon of mint, and allow to boil for one minute (overboiling will make the drink bitter). Strain and sweeten to taste.

Ru'a' (puff pastry): Sandwich two or three layers of puff pastry sheets with well-spiced ground beef or crumbled cottage cheese, saturate with ghee and bake in the oven.

Tahina (sesame paste): Thin the paste in water and mix thoroughly with lemon juice, cumin, and salt. Option: add
crushed garlic and finely chopped onion.

Ta'miya (bean cakes): Stew crushed broad beans overnight, then
drain and mince with fresh dill, coriander, onions, garlic, parsley, and leek. Add cumin, cayenne pepper, salt,
and a pinch of sodium bicarbonate and mix thoroughly to a smooth consistency. Shape into small flat
rounds, sprinkle one side with sesame seeds and deep
fry.

Tamr hindi (tamarind): Soak in water, then boil and filter—the
seed mass can be used in several boilings to make a
larger quantity. Sweeten to taste and drink hot or chill
before serving.

Tirmis (lupine): Soak the lupine seeds overnight, drain, add fresh
water, and simmer for seven to ten minutes. Drain,
rinse with cold water, and soak again for two to three
days, changing the water every twelve hours. By this
time, the seeds should be soft and should have lost
their bitter taste. Add salt and soak again for twenty-
four to thirty-six hours, repeating the above procedure
every twelve hours. Drain and serve.

'Ul'as (colocasia or taro): Peel, dice, and soak in warm water and
vinegar. Cut beef into small cubes and parboil with
onions, then add drained colocasia and seasoning and

simmer. Boil chopped coriander leaves in a small
amount of beef broth, mash or whirl in a blender with
crushed garlic and add to boiling stew.

Wara' 'inab (stuffed vine leaves): Spread open the boiled leaves
and add the filling—rice, ground beef, onions, salt and
pepper. Fold over and roll tightly. Place stuffed leaves
in a pot, then add cooking oil and hot water to cover
and cook over a moderate flame.

Yansun (aniseed): Boil one cup of water with half a teaspoon of
aniseed powder for one or two minutes until the water
absorbs the fragrance. Strain and sweeten to taste.